ENGINEERING LAW, DESIGN LIABILITY, and PROFESSIONAL ETHICS

— An Introduction for Engineers —

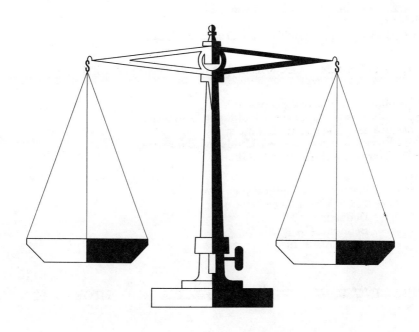

Rebecca J. Morton

PROFESSIONAL PUBLICATIONS, INC.

Belmont, CA 94002

ACKNOWLEDGMENT

"Typical Code of Ethics," found on page 77, reprinted from publication 1102, "Code of Ethics for Engineers," National Society of Professional Engineers, 1420 King Street, Alexandria, VA 22314.

In the ENGINEERING REVIEW MANUAL SERIES

Engineer-In-Training Review Manual
    Engineering Fundamentals Quick Reference Cards
    Mini-Exams for the E-I-T Exam
    E-I-T Index Card Of Figures and Tables
Civil Engineering Reference Manual
    Civil Engineering Quick Reference Cards
    Civil Engineering Sample Examination
    Civil Index Card of Figures and Tables
    Civil Engineering Review Course on Cassettes
    Seismic Design for the Civil P.E. Exam
    Timber Design for the Civil P.E. Exam
Structural Engineering Practice Problem Manual
Mechanical Engineering Review Manual
    Mechanical Engineering Quick Reference Cards
    Mechanical Engineering Sample Examination
    Mechanical Index Card of Figures and Tables
    Mechanical Engineering Review Course on Cassettes
Electrical Engineering Review Manual
Chemical Engineering Review Manual
    Chemical Engineering Practice Exam Set
Land Surveyor Reference Manual
Metallurgical Engineering Practice Problem Manual
Petroleum Engineering Practice Problem Manual
Expanded Interest Tables
Engineering Law, Design Liability, and Professional Ethics

In the ENGINEERING CAREER ADVANCEMENT SERIES

How to Become a Professional Engineer
The Expert Witness Handbook—A Guide for Engineers
Getting Started as a Consulting Engineer
Intellectual Property Protection—A Guide for Engineers
E-I-T/P.E. Course Coordinator's Handbook

Distributed by: Professional Publications, Inc.
               1250 Fifth Avenue
               Department 77
               Belmont, CA 94002
               (415) 593-9119

ENGINEERING LAW, DESIGN LIABILITY, AND PROFESSIONAL ETHICS

Printed in the United States of America

ISBN: 0-932276-37-7

Professional Publications, Inc.
1250 Fifth Avenue, Belmont, CA 94002

Current printing of this edition (last number) 8 7 6

PREFACE

Engineers and design professionals are affected greatly by the legal and ethical environment in which they operate. Engineers start design projects with consulting or employment contracts, work throughout those projects trying to avoid ethical entanglements, and finish facing an indefinite period of liability for their work.

This publication puts the subjects of engineering law, ethics, and liability into perspective by describing the important terms and concepts in layman's language. And, although there is no substitute for a lawyer, there is also little reason for engineers to be unfamiliar with such important legal terms as *discovery proceedings, contributory negligence,* and *collateral promise.*

This book started out as a primer for engineers preparing for their professional engineering examinations. However, its down-to-earth writing style, modular organization, and more than 120 case studies and practice problems make it ideal for any course in which contract law, ethics, and design liability are covered.

TABLE OF CONTENTS

PART I: ENGINEERING LAW

Engineering is a profession that affects most areas of human life in one way or another, with disciplines drawn from every scientific field of study. The civil engineer designs and constructs large structures like dams, bridges, and mass transportation systems; the mechanical engineer builds machines, ranging from toasters to space shuttles; the chemical engineer develops new materials and pharmaceuticals; the electrical engineer creates communications systems and energy generation systems. By applying modern technological developments, these and other engineering disciplines are constantly exploring ways to supply materials and services needed by society to function smoothly.

The consulting professional engineer is in a position of responsibility to guarantee that the products he or she creates are safe and efficient. To this end, society has established a set of laws binding the engineer. These laws have much in common with the laws that bind most human activity.

1. GENERAL LEGAL PRINCIPLES

Laws have evolved over the course of human history, and, consequently, the meaning of the word "law" is different in different contexts. For example, a law that states that a building must meet certain standards of construction is a very specific law designed to provide consistency in construction quality. A law that states that a company supplying energy to a community is responsible for the safety of the delivery of that energy is binding the company in a more general sense to safeguard the lives of the community it serves.

The specifics of law vary from culture to culture, but in every culture it is both an ideal and an institution. That is, law is the philosophy of what the society feels is the right and proper way to behave, and it is also a formalized code of conduct, making each citizen liable to specific punishments for disobeying specific laws. As a society evolves, so do that society's attitudes towards behavior; law is, therefore, constantly changing. In general, law can be divided into several categories.

Natural Laws. These are the principles that man has discovered to explain the physical phenomena of the universe. Scientists discover patterns of behavior in the physical world, and from this knowledge they are able to predict how material things will behave in the future. These physical laws are not created by man, but discovered by him through observation of the world around him.

Customs. In much the same way that natural laws are observed patterns of behavior in the physical world, customs are the observable patterns of behavior within a society that members of that society tend to follow. The origins of most customs are largely unknown and seldom questioned. They exist in primitive societies in the absence of a formal legal system in the form of tribal customs. In more advanced societies that have a formal legal system, customs are modes of behavior handed down from generation to generation and imply a moral obligation to conform.

PROFESSIONAL PUBLICATIONS, INC., P.O. Box 199, San Carlos, CA 94070

Subsets of society, such as trades or businesses, also develop customs that only apply to their particular types of activities, as, for example, when certain words acquire technical meanings that are different from the ordinary definitions.

Common Law. Historically, common law is the law originating in England and handed down through the English-speaking culture. This law is based primarily on historical precedence, and, as such, is in many ways similar to customs since it is based on tradition and consensus. Its authority comes from the courts; a decision reached in one case is considered a basis for deciding similar cases. This is the doctrine of *stare decisis,* more commonly known as *precedent* or *case law.* This aspect of common law provides some flexibility because it is open to interpretation. In the United States, there is a federal system that prescribes standards, but the individual states are free to interpret these standards in the light of regional customs and common law.

Statutory Law. Statutory law is legislated law; that is, it is created by a legislative body as a very specific action. As opposed to common law, statutory law is written down and prescribes particular actions that apply to specific situations. These laws, known as *statutes,* are upheld and interpreted by courts created by the processes prescribed by the legislature. Statutes may modify, reverse, or abolish common law doctrines on the same subject, and may themselves be changed or abolished by legislative action.

Municipal Law. Municipal law is a subclass of statutory law, and is the body of statutes passed by local governments. A municipality is a town, city, or village, and its statutes are generally referred to as *municipal ordinances.* Municipal law is administered through the local municipal system. These laws vary a great deal and are generally concerned with such things as traffic laws, zoning ordinances, public gatherings, and disturbances of the peace.

Constitutional Law. Constitutional law is based on the Constitution of the United States. It is a set of rules designed to define and control areas of governmental action and secure fundamental rights for the individual citizen. It is also concerned with the maintenance of the federal system and its relationship to state governments. Constitutional law generally involves Supreme Court decisions that interpret the federal Constitution.

Administrative Law. Administrative law is a large body of law based upon decisions, rulings, and regulations of various federal, state, and local agencies other than legislatures and courts. These agencies make rulings that affect public life, and regulate such things as business and industry, immigration, and environmental concerns. Examples of such agencies are the Occupational Safety and Health Administration and the Environmental Protection Agency. Administrative law is a combination of constitutional law, statutory law, case law, and agency rules and regulations. Although cases involving administrative law are ordinarily administered through the independent agencies, disputes are handled through the regular court system.

PROFESSIONAL PUBLICATIONS, INC., P.O. Box 199, San Carlos, CA 94070

A. Law in the United States

Law in the United States can broadly be defined as a rule of human conduct agreed upon through a consensus of legislation. Each citizen has the responsibility to obey these laws. Failure to do so produces legal consequences also defined by legislation and enforced by the courts. In return, each citizen is guaranteed certain individual rights that are protected by the Constitution.

The legal system in the United States is a system of law that is based on common law, but which has become heavily codified. It is characterized by the parallel systems of federal and state laws. The federal system is based on the Constitution and is concerned with questions of the relationship between the government and the people, and between the government and other nations. The state systems are based on the individual state constitutions and are more concerned with the details of how the law is to be administered. Local laws are aimed at prescribing individual behavior as it relates to the local community.

Law is created and administered by many different legislative bodies, existing in a hierarchy beginning with the federal government and extending down through state and local governments. Laws are enforced at the various levels by agents of the individual governments. In very broad terms, the federal courts are responsible for upholding the individual freedoms granted by the Constitution. The majority of cases are decided in state and municipal courts. The structure and working of these judicial systems vary a great deal between the states.

B. Sources of Law

The basis on which all law in this country is established is the United States Constitution, composed mainly of the Bill of Rights and Supreme Court decisions. The Bill of Rights is the guarantor of personal liberty, and no law can be enacted by any other legislative body or agency that contradicts it. The Constitution is intended to protect people against the government, not from other people.

The Supreme Court interprets the law established by the Constitution as it applies to specific rulings. It also has the power, granted it by the Constitution, to regulate interaction between the states; this has had a major impact on the regulation of interstate commerce. The Supreme Court also hears appeal cases when a federal or state law is questioned on the grounds of its agreement or disagreement with the Constitution.

The United States legislature, composed of Congress and the House of Representatives, is empowered to establish federal laws that apply to all states if the power to grant such a law is expressly given it by the Constitution. These statutes form the large body of federal law. The legislature also describes how the laws are to be administered through the system of federal district courts, courts of appeal, and the Supreme Court. There are 86 federal district courts in the United States that hear cases of federal law and appeals from the state courts.

Each state has its own constitution, usually modeled on the federal Constitution. These describe the organization of the state government and the procedures for creating and enforcing laws through the establishment of a

PROFESSIONAL PUBLICATIONS, INC., P.O. Box 199, San Carlos, CA 94070

state court system. Each state also has a large body of statutes expressing the common law tradition and defining the relationship of the state to other states and to the federal government.

Legislative bodies exist within each state, and they have the power to pass state laws and administer justice through a court system. State law is required to follow and uphold federal law. Likewise, local governments have the power to create and administer law, but cannot override state or federal statutes.

Administrative agencies exist at all levels of government. They create laws that apply to their specific areas, such as interstate commerce or labor relations. Many of their decisions are reached in an informal process, with hearings generally held before agency employees, but often disputes are heard in the federal district and appellate courts. Case law is quite prevalent in this area -- what has been decided and upheld in previous cases will determine the outcome of agency decisions.

C. Legal Relations

Every citizen has a role to play in the legal system. The system is, after all, designed to protect and make life easier for each member of society. Laws define people's rights, obligations, and their relationships to the government and to each other in a legal sense.

- A *legal right* is generally a capacity or interest that is recognized and protected by law.

- A *legal duty* is an obligation that is imposed or recognized by law.

- A *power* is an ability to do an act, or behave in a certain manner.

For example, suppose that Smith and Jones have entered into a valid contract. Smith has a "right" to obtain performance from Jones, and Jones has a "duty" to Smith to perform that act. Jones has the "power" to breach his contract with Smith, but we do not ordinarily say that Jones has the "right" to breach the contract.

Legal rights can further be classified as primary and secondary. *Primary rights* exist independently of any individual action; a person is entitled to these primary rights solely because a person is a member of society. According to common law principles, every person has a right to be secure in his person and property, and every other person owes him the duty not to violate this right.

Secondary rights are created by individual actions that are not required by law. An example is the contractual agreement between two parties, and the rights and legal duties defined by the contract are enforceable only against a particular person or class of persons under circumstances defined by the contract.

The legal concepts and classifications discussed here are the basic tools for analyzing legal problems. In any dispute, it is important to be able to classify the issues. Such classification may be according to subject matter,

PROFESSIONAL PUBLICATIONS, INC., P.O. Box 199, San Carlos, CA 94070

parties, or chronology to determine which laws apply to a given problem.

2. CONTRACTS

Contracts form the basis of most people's everyday legal activity. In the context of an engineer's professional life, contractual agreements are the basis upon which the engineer's work rests, whether it's an agreement for a particular piece of work or an employment contract with a firm, detailing the extent of individual liability and individual ownership of original work.

In its simplest sense, a contractual relationship is an agreement between two parties that is enforceable in a court of law. It is a promise by one person to another to do or not to do something in return for something else. *Contract law* is the enforcement of such promissory obligations, administered primarily by the state. The law differs in detail from state to state, but the basic procedures of contract law are fairly standard.

Contracts need not necessarily be in writing to be legally binding, as long as there is an implied intent to enter into a contractual agreement that is recognized by law. Such an agreement must meet several basic requirements:

   - It must be voluntary for all parties concerned.
   - It must be an exchange of goods or services.
   - All parties must have legal capacity.
   - The purpose of the contract must be legal.

There are many steps involved in forming and carrying out a contract. Before describing the procedure of creating and discharging contractual agreements, some preliminary definitions and concepts need to be introduced.

A. What Comprises a Contract?

A contract is a promise or a set of promises, the performance of which the law in some way recognizes as a duty, and, if breached, the law provides compensation to the injured party. A contract can also be described as an agreement, or the manifestation of mutual assent, a "meeting of the minds," between two or more legally competent parties that the law courts will enforce.

In order to be enforceable, a contract requires several prominent features to be present. These are: offer, acceptance, and consideration. These three features usually develop from a promise.

Promise. A promise is an expression, no matter how expressed, made by one person that leads another person reasonably to expect a particular act from the promisor. Such an expression is a promise whether enforceable by law or not. It is a guarantee by one person that something shall or shall not happen.

Offer. For a promise to be considered an offer in the legal sense, it must be clear, definite, and specific, with no room for ambiguity or misunderstanding. An offer is an act by a person that gives another person the legal

PROFESSIONAL PUBLICATIONS, INC., P.O. Box 199, San Carlos, CA 94070

power to create a contract. It is the basis of any contract, and must be explicitly made to a person or group of persons, and clear as to its terms and intent. When an offer is accepted by another person, it becomes a contract.

Acceptance. An acceptance is the agreement by a person to accept an offer made by another. Until such an agreement is made, no contract legally exists. As opposed to an offer, which must be explicit, an acceptance can be implied by the performance of the act requested by the offer. Both offer and acceptance must be voluntary acts; a contract cannot be forced on anyone.

Consideration. A contract must be supported by consideration. Consideration for a promise may be an act or the forbearance of an act, or the promise of such an act, or the creation, modification, or destruction of a legal relationship. Consideration may be given to the promisor or to some other person.

Consideration is a necessary element of any contract; a promise is not enforceable unless it is an agreement to exchange things of value. For example, if Smith and Jones enter into a contract in which Smith promises to pay Jones a sum of money for the performance of a service, both the money and the service are considerations.

It does not matter to the courts if the exchange is based on equal value or not; the promise to make the exchange is the legally binding contract. In addition, a contract cannot be made on a consideration unless the consideration is to be performed in the future -- past acts or payments are not legally binding.

B. Classification of Contracts

There are several methods normally used to classify contracts. These various classifications may overlap and are not necessarily mutually exclusive. Contracts may be classified, for example, as formal or informal, as unilateral or bilateral, as executory or executed. Other classifications are possible and several will be mentioned in this section.

Formal Contracts. Formal contracts are generally negotiable instruments, written documents that are used as a means of exchange and credit in the place of money. They are unconditional contracts in that the exchange of money is not based on the condition of some other requirement being met. A negotiable instrument usually requires that a sum of money be paid to a certain person at a certain time, no matter what. Most people have a private checking account drawn on a bank; their checks are negotiable instruments instructing the bank to pay money to another person when the check is presented.

Some other examples of negotiable instruments are promissory notes, which are written promises made by one person to pay a sum of money to another person at a certain time, and bills of exchange, which are similar to bank checks, but are used primarily in business and commerce, and are drawn on an individual or firm, rather than a bank.

Another type of formal contract is a *recognizance,* which is an acknowledgment in court by the recognizer that he is bound to make a certain payment

PROFESSIONAL PUBLICATIONS, INC., P.O. Box 199, San Carlos, CA 94070

unless a specified condition is performed. This is most commonly the condition of appearing for arraignment, and the recognizance is referred to as bail.

A type of formal contract that is no longer very much in existence, and has been completely abolished by some states, is the *contract under seal.* It was once the case that a promisor could affix his wax seal to a written promise and under common law this would be taken as a guarantee that a legally sufficient consideration was being offered, and the promise would become legally binding. As the wax seal became less prominent as a means of identification, being replaced with the written signature, this type of contract fell out of use.

Informal Contracts. All other types of contracts fall under the category of informal. This includes such things as purchase contracts, leases, and employment contracts. Primary to the business world is the contract to perform a service, be it a simple repair job or the construction of a home or office building. Also important in business is the contract to enter into partnership or create a corporation.

Executory Contracts. An executory contract is one that has not been fulfilled by either party or has been only partially performed by both parties.

Executed Contracts. An executed contract is one that has been completely fulfilled. It may also be a contract that has been performed by one party who now has a right to the payment of money from the other party.

Bilateral Contracts. A bilateral contract is one in which two parties have both made a promise to the other. Each party is both a promisor and a promisee. That is, there has been an agreement to exchange one thing for another.

Unilateral Contracts. A unilateral contract is one in which the promisor does not receive a promise as consideration for his promise, but instead receives an act or a service. The act may be an acceptance of the offer. For example, Smith says to Brown, "I promise to pay you $100.00 tomorrow if you will paint my house today." Brown immediately paints the house, thereby manifesting assent, accepting the offer, and creating a unilateral contract.

Express, Implied, and Quasi- Contracts. The distinction between express, implied, and quasi- contracts involves no difference in legal effect, but refers only to the way in which the contract is created.

An *express contract* is one in which all the terms of the contract are agreed upon and expressed in words, either oral or written.

An *implied contract* is one in which the agreement between the parties is inferred wholly or partly from conduct that indicates to the promisee that the promisor intended to make a promise. For example, Tom goes into a market where he has an account and sees a box of apples marked "15 cents each." He picks up an apple, holds it so the clerk can see it, the clerk nods, and Tom goes out with the apple. Tom has contracted to pay 15 cents for the apple. This is an implied contract.

A *quasi-contract* is not a true contract, since it is not based on the apparent intent of the parties, nor do quasi-contracts involve promises. A

PROFESSIONAL PUBLICATIONS, INC., P.O. Box 199, San Carlos, CA 94070

quasi-contract is based on a relationship created by law, such as marriage, with the obligations of a contract. At common law, these obligations are enforced in the same form of action as a contract. For example, if Henry's wife is justifiably separated from him and charges necessary clothing and food to Henry, he is bound to pay for them under a quasi-contractual obligation.

A quasi-contract also results when one person is in the possession of property belonging to another. Quasi-contractual obligations are implied contracts recognized by law to prevent one person from being unjustly enriched at the expense of another.

Joint, Several, and Joint and Several Contracts. If there are more than one promisor or promisee, a contract can take several forms to determine who is responsible for every and all parts of the contract. The wording of a contract with multiple promisors or promisees is very important, and it can have a great impact on the outcome of a breach of contract suit.

A *joint contract* is made when two or more persons promise the same performance to the same promisee as a single party; i.e., the contract is phrased "we promise...". If not stated otherwise, a contract with multiple parties on either side is assumed to be a joint contract. In a simple joint contract, all promisors are liable for the complete fulfillment of the contract. There is a single promise that may be fulfilled by any one of the promisors, but if there is a dispute over the contract, all promisors must be sued.

A *several contract* is made when separate performances are promised by more than one promisor to the same promisee; each promisor is liable only for his individual promise. For example, if Smith and Jones both sign a paper reading "Each of us guarantees to Brown that he shall be duly repaid the $100.00 which he has lent Sam," then Smith and Jones are severally bound, but only one of them need perform the promise. If the contract is not completed satisfactorily, Brown may sue either Smith or Jones separately or the two of them together.

In a *joint and several contract,* two or more parties make a joint contract, but also state explicitly that they are individually liable for the completion of the contract. This differs from separate promises in a several contract mainly because of the factor of cumulative liability. For example, Smith, Jones, and Brown all sign a contract saying: "I promise to pay White $100.00 in 30 days." This creates joint and several duties on the part of Smith, Jones, and Brown, meaning that each of them is responsible for paying White $100.00. If the promise is not fulfilled, White may sue any of the three individually, or he may sue them all in a single action, but he will never be able to claim more than $100.00.

When a joint contract is disputed due to the failure of joint promisors to fulfill their promise, judgment must be against all of the defendants originally jointly bound. The only exception is if one of the original group of promisors (known as the *joinder*) is for some reason (such as death or lack of jurisdiction) unable to be sued. If, however, there is no objection from the joinder, any subset of the joinder may be sued. Judgment against one or more joint promisors discharges the joint duty of other joint promisors. The several duty of a promisor in a several or joint and several contract is not discharged by judgment for or against one or more of the others.

PROFESSIONAL PUBLICATIONS, INC., P.O. Box 199, San Carlos, CA 94070

Oral and Written Contracts. Not all contracts must be in writing to be enforceable. Many of our daily contractual agreements are not written agreements, such as short-term services or repairs. Sometimes a memorandum signed by one party is sufficient to create an enforceable contract, but interpretation is tricky and varies from state to state.

The *statute of frauds* states explicitly what types of contracts must be in writing. It originated in England common law with the passing in 1676 of *An Act of Prevention of Frauds and Perjuries*. The intention of the act was to prevent fraud resulting from perjury when a contract was not in writing. Each state now has its own version, but in general they require the same types of contracts to be in writing. These are:

- Promises by an administrator or executor of an estate to cover the debts of the estate from his own property.

- Any promise by one person to pay for the debts, damages, or misconduct of another person. This must be a direct promise to become a creditor. For example, if John says to Lynn, "Loan Sam $5.00 and I will pay you back if Sam doesn't," this promise is covered under the statute of frauds, and so must be in writing. But if John had said, "Give Sam $5.00 worth of goods and I will pay you for it," this would be a direct promise to pay money to Lynn. Because it is not a promise to cover the debts of another person, it does not come under the statute of frauds, so it would not need to be in writing to be enforceable. In general, if the primary purpose is for the benefit of the promisor, then it is usually a direct rather than a collateral promise (as is a co-signed loan), and it therefore does not come under the statute of frauds.

- An agreement not to be fulfilled within a year or a lifetime. This really means agreements that cannot or might not be performed within a year. If there is a possibility that full performance may be obtained within a year, the statute of frauds does not apply. For example, if John promised to support Bill for life, it would not come under the statute of frauds because John might die within a year, whereas if he promised to support Bill for two years, it would come under the statute of frauds because it cannot be completed until two years have elapsed.

- A contract for the sale or lease of real property.

- A contract for the sale of goods of substantial value (usually over $500).

The statute of frauds does not specify that if any of the above types of contracts are not in writing that they are illegal. But if they are disputed, they might not be enforceable in a court of law. Other types of oral contracts might still be enforceable because they do not come under the statute of frauds.

Voidable, Void, and Unenforceable Contracts. Contracts can be non-binding, usually due to circumstances surrounding their creation. Non-binding contracts are classified as voidable, void, and unenforceable.

PROFESSIONAL PUBLICATIONS, INC., P.O. Box 199, San Carlos, CA 94070

A *voidable contract* is one in which one or more of the parties may have the right to choose to honor the contract or to nullify it because of some defect in their legal obligations. Until the party decides one way or the other, it remains a legally binding contract. The cases in which a contract is voidable are:

- Contracts made by minors (those under 21). The minor can choose to hold the other party to the contract, accepting the legal obligation created by the contract, or may void the contract.

- Contracts induced by fraud or misrepresentation. Misrepresentation means that there has been a false representation of a material fact. This false representation must be intentional and must result in damages. The party victimized by the fraud may choose to void his contractual obligations and not be subject to penalty.

- Contracts made under duress or undue influence, or by mistake. In this case, an agreement is made as the result of something other than the complete and mutual assent of both parties. Duress means some sort of force, be it physical, mental, or emotional. Undue influence means taking advantage of a position of trust or confidence, or the distress of another. A mistake is a valid reason for voiding a contract only if one party knows or should have known of the mistake made by the other party; a mistake doesn't mean simply making a bad deal.

A *void contract* is one that is not legally binding or enforceable under any circumstances. The law does not give a remedy for the breach of such contract, nor does it otherwise recognize the contract as creating a legal obligation. In most cases, this is a contract for an act which is itself illegal, such as a gambling contract.

An *unenforceable contract* is a valid contract, but one in which the binding agreement for some reason cannot be proven by either of the parties. These are usually cases that have violated the statue of frauds. It can also mean a contract that is not enforceable because of the statute of limitations, which sets a time limit on when the contract can be enforced. Both the statute of frauds and the statute of limitations vary from state to state and for different kinds of contracts.

C. The Formation of Contracts

As described earlier, not every agreement is a contract. A contract is formed only when certain procedures have been followed. To be legally binding, a contract must include the following elements:

- An agreement must be reached between two or more persons as to the terms of the contract. The terms must be stated in a definite, unambiguous manner.

- There must be a definite consideration of some value for the agreement.

- The contracting parties must be legally competent.

PROFESSIONAL PUBLICATIONS, INC., P.O. Box 199, San Carlos, CA 94070

- The contract must be for something that is itself legal.

The agreement between the contracting parties is the most important element in a contract, but the agreement, regardless of how it is expressed, is qualified by the apparent intent of the parties, implied behavior, and other circumstances that might alter the interpretation of either party's behavior. In other words, the parties to a contract are bound by their conduct towards one another, whether a promise is expressly stated or implied through some act or relationship. This is the *objective theory* of contract law.

A person's subjective intent cannot be taken into account in a court of law. That is, what a person meant to promise doesn't matter; what his behavior led the other person to believe he meant is what he is held to. This objective theory is important simply because it would be too easy for a person to escape liability by showing that he had no real intention to create a contract. Contract law is primarily designed to protect the individual in his business dealings with others.

The Agreement -- Offer and Acceptance. A legal contract is the result of an agreement between two parties. An agreement is made up of an offer and an acceptance.

An *offer* is the first step towards creating a contract. It must be definite and certain if it is to be the basis of a legal contract. An offer to "do whatver you say for $100" is not a legal offer, because its terms are too vague and the discharge of a contract based on such an offer could not be determined. Neither is an invitation to seek an agreement, such as "Let's get together and see what I could do for you in exchange for $100." An offer must state exactly what is offered and what is expected, if anything, in return.

There are cases where intent is misunderstood, even if the wording of the offer is very explicit. For example, an offeror might offer to sell a car for $300 when he actually meant to ask $400 for it. If his offer of $300 is accepted, he is legally bound to his offer. This falls under the rule of the objective theory of contracts, which states that it is outward behavior rather than inward intent that is important when forming an agreement.

This does not necessarily mean that a vague offer cannot lead to a legal contract. If the original offer is ambiguous, it could still lead to a legal contract if both parties agree on what the offer means. For example, an offer to sell goods need not be specific as to the price of the goods if the parties agree to accept the current market price of the goods at the time of delivery. This is only applicable to goods for which a market price is readily ascertainable. If, at the time of delivery, the parties cannot agree on a price, the court will set a price based on the current market price of the goods.

But in most cases, if certain terms of the offer are left open, such as the amount, grade, quality, or kind of goods to be used, the offer is not sufficiently definite. An agreement based on such an offer would be hard to uphold in court because it would be hard to determine if the agreement had been met. For example, if a company makes an offer to supply a contractor with all the goods that he might need, the offer is probably sufficient as to the amount because the contractor only needs so much for a

PROFESSIONAL PUBLICATIONS, INC., P.O. Box 199, San Carlos, CA 94070

particular job. However, an offer to supply him with all the goods he might want is not sufficiently definite because it is based on a subjective demand.

An offer must be made to a particular person or group of people. An exception to this is a reward offered by someone for the return of something; this is an open offer to the public at large. The offer must be communicated to the offeree and accepted by that offeree before it is a legal contract; no contract can exist unless there is communication between the contracting parties. If Smith and Jones make independent offers to each other and they cross in the mail, there is no contract possible until they know of each other's offer. There is still no contract if a third party were to tell one of them of the other's intentions.

In addition to being definite, an offer must present a contractual intent. That is, the offer must be worded such that it is apparent that on acceptance, the offer will become a legally binding contract. This is distinct from an invitation to accept offers. Advertisements for the sale of articles fall under this heading. They are invitations for offers -- the buyer makes an offer to buy and the seller, who made the advertisement, accepts it if he wishes.

Contractual intent must be for the creation of a legal rather than a social obligation. A dinner invitation is a social offer, and no legal contract is formed by the acceptance of it. An offer to perform moral duties, such as to care for a sick aunt, is not enforceable by law either. Political promises also fall into this category, and are unenforceable.

An *acceptance* must be made to an offer before the agreement can be legally binding; that is, the offeree must agree to the proposed contract. In its simplest sense, an acceptance is the requested return by the offeree of the offer, and in many cases, the offeree's assent is implied by performing the requested act.

He must, however, have had prior knowledge of the offer; coincidental acceptance does not create a contract. For example, in the case of a public offer of a reward for the return of a lost item, if the return of the item is made by someone who did not know of the reward, there is no contract. A person cannot accept an offer of which he is ignorant, but if the person has knowledge of the offer, acceptance is shown when he gives the requested return.

The offeror has the power to specify a time period at the end of which the offer is no longer valid. If an offeree sends his acceptance too late, it becomes a counter-offer which must then be accepted by the original offeror. If the offeror does not specify a time within which the offer must be accepted, the acceptance must still come within a reasonable time. If no specific time period is stated, the offeror must notify the offeree that the acceptance has come too late, if such is the case.

The offeror may also stipulate the mode of acceptance of the offer. If not explicitly stated, the mode may be implied by the mode of the offer. For example, if the offer is made through the mail, it is implied, but not legally required, that the acceptance be made through the mail. Or the acceptance might be required to be sent through the mail regardless of how the offer was made. If the offeror does stipulate that the acceptance must be mailed, the contract becomes legal when the offeree posts the acceptance, unless the offeror specifically states that the acceptance must be received before the contract becomes binding. In this case, if the acceptance is lost in the mail and never received by the offeror, no contract is made.

If the acceptance is made by some other means than what is stipulated in the offer, no contract is made until the acceptance is received and accepted by the offeror. If an offer is made by telegram, and the acceptance sent by mail, it is effective only when received; whereas if the offer were made by mail and the mode of acceptance were not stipulated, the contract would become effective when the acceptance was dropped in the mailbox. The offeror has the right to refuse the contract until the acceptance has been communicated in the proper form.

In all cases, the acceptance must be communicated to the offeror in some way, either by a formal acceptance or by the performance of the requested act. A lack of response cannot be construed as an acceptance unless such a mode of acceptance is agreed upon in advance by the offeror and offeree. The offeror cannot place the burden on the offeree to expressly reject an offer under penalty. That is, the offeror cannot say, "If I don't hear from you within 10 days, we have a contract." In some cases, acceptance can be inferred from acts on the part of the offeree. A common example of this is a visit to a doctor's office -- you agree to accept the doctor's offer of services and are legally bound by that agreement.

An offer can be *revoked* before an acceptance is made under certain conditions. If the offer was made to a specific offeree, that person must be notified directly of the revocation of the offer. It is usually standard to notify the offeree at his place of business. The revocation does not become effective until this notice is received. In some cases, if the offeree learns indirectly of the revocation, this counts as a legal rescinding of the offer.

If the offer has been made to the public, as in the case of a reward, the offer must be withdrawn through the same means by which the offer was made, such as a newspaper ad or public flyers.

If the offer expressly states that the offer is to remain valid for a specific period of time, the offeror may still revoke the offer at any time before the original period has elapsed, unless there is a binding option. An *option* is an agreement between the offeror and offeree to keep the offer open for a specified period of time. For example, if Smith made an offer to Jones to sell him some materials at a certain price and as part of the offer agreed to keep the offer open for two weeks, and before the two week period was up, Smith sold the material to someone else, he would be legally bound to his offer to Jones, even though Jones had not formally accepted his offer.

If the offeree makes a counter-offer or requests substantial modifications to the original offer, this constitutes a rejection of the offer. At this point, the original offer is no longer valid, and a new offer is negotiable.

If the offeror is proven to be insane or dies before completion of the agreement, the offer is no longer valid.

Consideration. A contract must be supported by *consideration*. Because a contract is by definition a voluntary act, there must be some reason for the contracting promise. The contracting parties must agree to exchange things

PROFESSIONAL PUBLICATIONS, INC., P.O. Box 199, San Carlos, CA 94070

that are of value to themselves. Whether or not the consideration exchanged is of any objective value is not necessarily a legal question. The test of the adequacy of the consideration is whether it incurs a legal detriment; that is, if a person does something that he is not legally required to do. Consideration can, therefore, also be defined as a detriment suffered or promised in exchange for an act or promise.

In a bilateral contract, a legal detriment is a promise to do something that the promisee is not legally bound to do, or to refrain from something that the promisee has a legal right to do. For example, if someone promises to give you $1,000 to stop smoking for a year, the consideration that person receives for his money could be construed to be the pleasure he gets from seeing you stop smoking. It could also be that he has stopped you from doing something that you have a legal right to do. He has received an act from you in exchange for his promise of payment.

To be valuable, the consideration does not necessarily have to have a monetary value; in the case above, the abstention from smoking has no monetary value, and in fact, there is no value to anyone other than the people involved in the agreement. But there is value from the point of view of its being an act that is not the inherent legal duty of a citizen. You have promised to do it in return for something else, or, in other words, you have given up a legal right for something else. Legal rights can be bargained for in much the same way as material goods.

A *gift* is not consideration. Both parties must in some way receive and give legal consideration. A promise to give someone something of value is not enforceable if nothing were to be returned to that person in exchange for the gift. If Bob says that he will buy his niece a new car when she graduates from college, it would not be an enforceable promise. Bob will not be receiving anything of legal value in exchange, and there will be no detriment suffered by his niece because she is not deprived of any legal right in exchange for the gift.

In some cases, however, a gift may be construed as a legally binding promise if the party to whom the promise was made relies upon that promise and as a result suffers some detriment. For example, if you were to suffer financial loss as the result of relying on someone else to provide what they promised or if substantial injustice would result from the promise not being kept, then the promise of the gift would constitute a legally binding agreement.

The equality of the value of the exchange is not necessarily of any legal concern, but if the values of the things exchanged are grossly disproportionate, the consideration may be discounted by the court and the contract made unenforceable. One of the few cases when the proportionate value of the exchange is considered is in cases of fraud, where one party has misled the other into believing that what they were receiving was of more value than it really was. This is more a case of misrepresentation than unequal consideration.

If a person can prove that the other party has committed fraud, he is released from the obligations created by the contract. *Fraud* is simply the false statement made knowingly of a material fact by one party that the other party relies upon and consequently suffers a financial or legal loss. The law does not provide counsel for making a smart bargain, but it does

PROFESSIONAL PUBLICATIONS, INC., P.O. Box 199, San Carlos, CA 94070

try to protect innocent people from being defrauded.

The promise to exchange things must be based on things that are to occur in the future. You cannot bargain on things that have already been done or exchanged. A promise to pay for services that have already been rendered cannot be enforced; the promise must be made before the services are rendered, and the promise to pay is the consideration exchanged for the services rendered. A promise made after the fact is known as *past consideration.*

In a situation where an act is being exchanged for payment, there is a *unilateral contract.* The promise to pay is the consideration given by the offeror, and the act is the consideration given in return by the offeree. In a *bilateral contract,* the two parties each perform an act for the other. In this case, a promise is made in return for a promise. For example, if Smith promises to paint Brown's house, and in return, Brown promises to wash Smith's car, they are creating a bilateral contract.

However, both promises must be definite; an illusory promise is not consideration. A frequent problem with contracts is that they are not really promises to exchange anything. Each party must be obligated to provide something to the other. If a person says, "Do this and I might do that," there is no contract, because there is no consideration, and no return promise.

Sometimes a contract will be made with only a nominal consideration. For instance, a father might sell his daughter a car for $1.00. This is actually a gift, but the transaction is made in the form of a contract so that the exchange will be a legal contract. This is necessary in cases when the consideration (in this case, a car) carries a legal title and is required by law to be exchanged through legal procedures.

The performance of an obligation under a pre-existing contract cannot be consideration for a new promise. You cannot promise to do something that you are already legally obligated to do and expect to receive consideration in exchange for it. For example, if John owes Jeff $100 and promises to pay him $75 on Tuesday as full payment, there is no legally binding promise. John still owes Jeff $100. However, if they make a new agreement in which Jeff forfeits his rights to the full $100 and John agrees to pay the $75 by Tuesday, then a valid contract may be formed. The new contract should include specifically the statement that this new contract cancels the old debt of $100.

Since consideration is usually the main content of any contractual agreement, the exchange of consideration must be definite and certain. There should be no ambiguity about what exactly is being exchanged. A contract cannot be based on something that is not tangible; you cannot promise someone that you will be "a good person" for a year if they will pay you $100, because the exchange would be based on a subjective appraisal of your behavior.

Each contract and each exchange is different. Consideration might be obvious in most cases, but not in others. In its most general sense, consideration is that thing, be it material or not, that you are receiving or giving in a mutual exchange. Consideration must be a bargained for exchange; it cannot be something you are naturally entitled to as a primary right, or something that someone offers to give you as a gift.

PROFESSIONAL PUBLICATIONS, INC., P.O. Box 199, San Carlos, CA 94070

Legal Capacity. Both parties to a contract must have the legal capacity to enter into a contract. Capacity is the ability to take recognized legal action. It is the responsibility of each contracting party to be sure that the other party has legal capacity to contract.

Those persons without legal capacity are minors, mentally incompetent persons, and drunken or drugged persons. An agreement made by persons classified as such result in a voidable contract. This is for the protection of the less capable; those contracting with such parties might still be held responsible for their contractual obligations.

- Minors. Some contracts entered into by minors may be enforceable, but for the most part they are voidable. The minor cannot be held liable, but if the other contracting party is an adult, he might be held to his part of the contract. The age of maturity in most states is 21.

- Mentally incompetent persons. Because one of the primary concepts of contracts is that of voluntary agreement between two parties, if one party is not capable of understanding what he is doing, such a contract would come under the heading of a contract made under duress or undue influence. A person must be declared mentally incompetent by the court. Temporary mental incapacity might in some cases also prevent an agreement from being a legally binding contract.

- Drunken or drugged persons. A contract made while a person is under the influence of alcohol or drugs is not legally binding. As in the case of mentally incompetent persons, the person's ability to comprehend what he is agreeing to is of primary importance. A person can be declared an habitual drunkard and therefore of diminished mental capabilities.

Legality. You cannot create a legally binding contract to do something that is illegal or against public policy. Since there is no clear definition of public policy, each case is judged individually as to the intent of the contract. Some examples of contractual agreements that are not enforceable because of the illegality of the consideration are:

- Contracts for the sale of public offices, public contracts, or the bribing of public officials.

- Contracts ousting a court's jurisdiction or compounding crimes, which usually applies to criminal rather than civil cases.

- Contracts encouraging litigation.

- Contracts for the commission of crimes or torts.

- Contracts tending to promote fraud or breach of trust, as when an engineer agrees with a contractor to use his influence to have a contract awarded to the contractor in exchange for a commission.

- Contracts in restraint of trade or competition.

PROFESSIONAL PUBLICATIONS, INC., P.O. Box 199, San Carlos, CA 94070

- Contracts involving usury, the charging of interest rates higher than the standard established by the state.

- Contracts injurious to public health or safety.

- Contracts establishing unlawful monopolies.

- Contracts with unlicensed people who are required to have licenses to practice.

Of course, the specificity of any agreement can almost always be called into question and interpreted in more than one way. The more precise you can make a contract, the less chance there is of it being called into dispute. But whenever two contracting parties cannot agree on the mutual satisfaction of the original promise, the dispute is taken into court, and a judge decides the case. He bases his decision on his knowledge of contract law and the large body of cases decided in the past. That is, he makes his decision based on precedent and the most likely agreement between the two parties given the specific circumstances.

D. The Interpretation of Contracts

Contracts are intended to provide a surety that one person upholds a legal promise to another. For this reason, the terms of the contract should convey the real intention of both parties toward one another. If one party does not perform as promised, the contract provides the other party legal recourse to receive compensation.

When there is a dispute over the completion of a contract, such as when one party claims that the other party has not met the contractual obligation, the courts must decide what the original agreement was and what is needed to satisfactorily complete the contract. If the contract is in writing, and the terms of the contract are very explicit, there is usually no problem in deciding who is at fault and what would comprise adequate compensation. But there is often a misunderstanding of the original agreement, and most cases that get to court are there because of some disagreement about the terms of the agreement.

There are guidelines established that the courts apply in the interpretation of contracts when there is a dispute. These are not legally binding rules, but ways to fairly and consistently determine the actual facts of the agreement. In any contract dispute, the primary role of the court is first to determine what the parties had contracted for in the first place before any ruling can be affected concerning the completion of each party's contractual obligations.

If the agreement is in writing, then the written terms will take priority over any other evidence introduced. This is the *parol evidence rule.* This rule states very generally that if there is a written agreement, then any testimony outside that written agreement does not have to be considered. This rule only applies when the written agreement is clearly intended as the complete agreement. In most contracts there is a *merger clause,* which states explicitly that the contract is the complete agreement. If there is a contradiction between the written terms of the contract and an oral agreement made between the parties, the written terms will prevail.

PROFESSIONAL PUBLICATIONS, INC., P.O. Box 199, San Carlos, CA 94070

If there is ambiguity in the wording of a written agreement, it will be interpreted in the light of the plain, usual, or literal meaning of the words. If, however, the words have a special meaning due to local usage or customs of a trade, or if there are technical words that have special meaning within the context of the contract, they will be interpreted as they apply. This relates to the parol evidence rule in that oral testimony may be allowed to explain ambiguity in a written document.

If there is some doubt about the meaning of a word in a contract, it is up to the contracting parties to agree on the interpretation of the wording within the context of the contract, and their agreement will be accepted by the court. If there is a dispute between the contracting parties as to the meaning of a word, the interpretation will be left up to the court, which is bound to judge in favor of the interpretation most commonly held, or most liable to make the contract valid.

In some cases, an ambiguity might create two possible interpretations of the terms of a contract. If one interpretation would render the contract void or such that it could not possibly be completed, it would be surrendered in favor of an interpretation that would make the contract valid and performable.

When a contract is disputed, and an interpretation must be made by the court before a decision can be reached regarding the fulfillment of the contract, the court will invariably interpret the contract in the favor of the contracting party. The party who prepared the contract, in many cases a business or insurance company, is at a disadvantage in a contract dispute. This is only in regards to the terms of the agreement, and does not necessarily affect the final decision regarding the satisfactory completion of the contract.

If a satisfactory interpretation of the terms of the contract cannot be determined, the contract will be considered unenforceable. It is always to the benefit of both parties that all terms of a contract are in writing and there is no misunderstanding between them.

E. The Modification of a Contract

A contract may be modified after it is agreed on if both parties agree to the modifications. Generally, if new terms are created, there must be new consideration. If not, then it is probably the case that the original contract is being rescinded by mutual agreement and a new contract is being formed.

The modification of a contract that is required to be in writing under the statute of frauds is also required to be in writing. An oral modification of such a contract is not binding, and, in effect, becomes a separate agreement. If the agreement made by the oral modification is disputed, it can be brought to court as a quasi-contract, but may not be allowed in the settlement of the original contract.

F. The Discharge of a Contract

A contract is said to be discharged when the agreement has been performed to the satisfaction of both parties. That is, both parties agree that they have each done what was originally required of them under the terms of the contract. When the contract is fully performed, it is discharged, and all rights and duties created under the contract are dissolved.

At any time, a contract may be discharged or altered if the contracting parties agree. A contract required to be in writing by the statute of frauds must be released by a written agreement.

A contract is discharged if it becomes impossible to perform it due to circumstances outside the control of the contracting parties. This could be due to several things. If the object of the contract were a piece of personal property, such as a house, and that property were destroyed by a natural disaster, the contract would no longer be binding. If the contract were for personal services that only a certain person could perform and that person were to die or otherwise be prevented from performing the contract, it would be discharged.

Extreme difficulty of executing the contract does not discharge it, even if it becomes more costly than originally anticipated. For example, if Jones has contracted to build a house for Brown for a certain price, and due to poor soil conditions, strikes, or difficulty in obtaining materials, the construction costs are higher than either Jones or Brown expected, Jones is still held to the original contract. If, however, there were contingency clauses in the contract to allow for modifications based on these unexpected happenings, it would be possible to modify the contract.

If the terms of the contract become impossible to complete, but there is still satisfactory completion, a contract is discharged if both parties agree. For example, if different materials than specified in the contract are substituted, but are considered of equal quality, that would be satisfactory completion. Or, if there has been a willful departure from the terms, as in the case where a house would be unsafe if built according to original terms, the contract could be discharged.

If an existing law changes, making the contract illegal, it is discharged. If only part of the contract is made illegal by changing legislation, the rest of it could remain binding. If a contract is made in a state where the contract would be considered void due to state laws, it will be considered void in other states, even if that state's laws were such that the contract would be legal. Some contracts may be dissolved by actions of the court, such as bankruptcy, public acts, or a declaration of war.

Breach of Contract. The above describes situations where a contract is discharged by agreement of the contracting parties or by the court. However, sometimes a contract is discharged because one party fails to perform his part of the contract. This is known as *breach of contract*. A breach may be partial or total.

A *total breach* is sometimes called a *material breach*, and it means that the injured party has not received a substantial part of the performance of the contract. The injured party is released from all duties on his part of the contract and may then sue for damages. A *partial breach* involves only the non-performance of a small part of the contract, and the injured party is only allowed to sue for damages stemming from that part of the agreement, and is not released from his part of the contract. There is no definitive way of deciding whether a breach is partial or total; each case must be decided individually by the court.

PROFESSIONAL PUBLICATIONS, INC., P.O. Box 199, San Carlos, CA 94070

If one party repudiates the contract, that is, announces that he does not intend to complete his part of the contract prior to the time he is required by the contract to perform his part, it is known as *anticipatory breach*. The injured party is then allowed to sue for total breach and is released from his obligations under the contract.

However, if a party wanted to bring suit for breach of contract because of the lack of satisfactory performance from the other party, the plaintiff would have to be in a situation to be able to perform his part of the contract, but be waiting for some action on the part of the other party. This is known as a *tender of performance* -- the plaintiff is being kept from performing his part of the contract because of the neglect of the other party. In this case, the plaintiff may decide to rescind the contract and sue only for the restitution of any monies dispensed by him in the performance of the contract.

The plaintiff may also sue for *damages*. Damages are the losses incurred by the plaintiff as a result of the non-performance of the contract.

- *General or compensatory damages* are awarded to make up for the injury that was sustained.

- *Special damages* are awarded for the direct financial loss due to the breach.

- *Nominal damages* are awarded when responsibility has been established but the amount of injury is so slight as to be inconsequential.

- *Punitive or exemplary damages* are awarded usually in tort cases as a punishment for the defendant.

- *Consequential damages* provide compensation for losses incurred by the plaintiff not directly related to the contract in question but as an indirect result of the breach.

In a breach of contract suit, punitive damages cannot be claimed. Nor can the plaintiff ask for compensation for mental anguish caused by the breach.

Damages may be money damages, either the actual cost of damages suffered by the plaintiff due to the breach of contract, or a reasonable amount when an exact amount cannot be determined.

If money damages are inadequate compensation, the plaintiff may ask for *specific performance,* in which case the court might order the defendant to perform the contractual obligation. Specific performance is an equitable remedy available to enforce the conveyance of land and in certain contracts relating to personal property where money damages will not do justice. For example, a buyer might want certain articles for sentimental or personal reasons, and substituting a similar article will not satisfy him. Specific performance cannot be applied in cases where the performance of the contract would entail hardship or injustice, or in cases of personal services, where the requirement of performance would constitute forced labor.

Liquidated damages are damages that are specified in the contract to insure

PROFESSIONAL PUBLICATIONS, INC., P.O. Box 199, San Carlos, CA 94070

that if the contract becomes disputed, the amount of damages are agreed upon in advance. If the damages specified in this way are deemed at the time of the lawsuit to be unreasonable, they are not enforceable. In general, a clause in the contract that specifies damages ahead of time is only a guideline; the case will be judged in light of what actual damages have been incurred by the plaintiff.

The plaintiff has the responsibility to minimize his damages if he has the opportunity. If the plaintiff foresees a breach, he cannot act in such a way as to increase the damages that he could sue for. If the court determines that he could have lessened his damages through prudent action, the judgment will probably be less than compensatory.

There is another way to settle breach of contract disputes without going to court. This is *arbitration.* If the parties agree, either ahead of time as a clause of the contract or at the time of the dispute, they can submit their claim to the American Arbitration Association. Decisions of the arbitrators can be as binding as the judgments of a court, and such decisions have the additional advantage of being faster and cheaper for all parties involved. However, a plaintiff who has a strong position may be at a disadvantage in an arbitration case.

When a breach of contract suit has been decided in court or by arbitration, the contract is discharged, and the duties and responsibilities are no longer binding.

G. The General Form of a Contract

Every contract should specify all the terms of the agreement. This will differ due to the specific circumstances of the offer and acceptance, but in general every contract should have the following clauses:

- An introduction to the agreement, with a title and the date.

- The name and address of all parties. If one of the parties is a corporation, it should be designated as such.

- The details of the agreement, including all promises to be performed, with details as to the type of work, the materials, specifications, etc., and all promises of payment, including amounts, installments, and interest rates.

- Supporting documents, such as drawings of plans, technical information, specifications, and statements of any conditions upon which the agreement hinges.

- The date and time of commencement and the expected time of completion.

- Payment. Exact dollar figures or easily ascertainable values are recommended.

- Liquidated damages for non-performance, arbitration agreements, and any other clauses to be enacted in the event of non-completion by one of the parties.

- Other general provisions of the agreement.

- Final clauses, signatures, witnesses, notary.

3. LIENS

A lien is a claim that one person holds against the real property of another as security for a debt or contractual obligation. The lien claimant has the right to retain the property until payment is secured, and he can have the property sold if the debt is not paid.

A lien usually must be secured, or *perfected,* by the claimant before he can claim the property as payment for the debt. This might involve simply filing notice in a public office. Once the claimant attaches property through the perfection of a lien, the lien is held against the property, even if the property is sold to another party.

For example, if Smith owns a piece of property and he owes Jones $1000, Jones could acquire a lien against the property to secure the payment of the loan. If Smith sells the property to Brown before paying his loan to Jones, then Jones could enforce the lien against Brown. However, if Jones had not secured the loan by acquiring a lien, then he would have no right to the property that now belongs to Brown. It is Brown's responsibility to see that there is no lien against the property before he buys it.

There are many types of liens, most of which are statutory liens, meaning that they are based on statutory law. Consequently, the lien laws vary a great deal from state to state.

- *Mechanic's liens* are liens to secure the payment of labor and materials provided for the improvement of property.

- *Judgments* are liens created by the court as the settlement of personal liability cases.

- *Tax liens* are liens created to secure the payment of overdue taxes.

- *Attachments* are liens created by the court for the duration of a lawsuit to prevent a party from selling land so that it cannot be claimed in a judgment.

A. Mechanic's Liens

A mechanic (i.e., a contractor) is one who provides labor or material towards the improvement of real property. *Real property* is land and buildings, distinguishable from *personal property,* which is something that can be easily moved by its owner. A mechanic can acquire a lien on the real property of another as security for any work or materials provided towards the improvement of that property. This is known as a mechanic's lien and is a guarantee to the worker that he can expect to be paid when he completes his work.

A mechanic's lien is primarily for the protection of the persons supplying

PROFESSIONAL PUBLICATIONS, INC., P.O. Box 199, San Carlos, CA 94070

labor or material on credit; it is the security for the "loan" of labor and material. Because they are adding to the the value of the property, mechanics are entitled to compensation from this added value. If the landowner does not pay for the work, he is obligated to sell the land in order to pay his debt.

When a person acquires a lien, he has a priority of payment over any lien acquired later. For example, if Smith begins some work on the property of Jones, and Jones then mortgages the property to Brown, who then hires Green to begin work, then Smith, Brown, and Green can all have liens against the property, but Smith has priority of payment over Brown and Green, and Brown has priority of payment over Green.

The point at which a mechanic's lien attaches to the property varies from state to state. In some states, the lien becomes valid when work begins, while in others it becomes valid when the contract is completed, while in still others it only becomes valid when a notice of the lien is filed in a public office.

There is usually a distinction in mechanic's lien laws between the contractor and the subcontractor. A *contractor* is hired by the landowner to oversee construction. The contractor then hires *subcontractors* to do particular portions of the work. Generally, the subcontractor is responsible to the contractor, not the landowner. In some states, a subcontractor has very limited powers of acquiring a lien, whereas in other states a landowner is responsible to all subcontractors regardless of the fulfillment of his duties toward the contractor.

If the landowner did not explicitly request particular improvements, a lien against his property might not be enforceable. Or if land is jointly owned, and only one owner approved the work, a lien cannot be attached to the shares of the other owners. In some states, the contractor must prove that the landowner explicitly contracted with him for the work. In other states, it is only necessary to prove that the landowner consented to the work, or was aware that the work was being done. If a legal agent of the landowner contracted for the work, the landowner is held responsible.

A tenant is not a legal agent of a landowner. Only if there is a special clause in the lease can a lien be attached to the property if work was orderd by a tenant without the landlord's consent. If, for example, a contractor provides labor or materials to a tenant for the construction of something which is removable from the property by the tenant, the contractor cannot attach a lien to the landlord's property. A great deal of litigation develops because of the ordering of work by tenants, and in most cases, the lien cannot be enforced.

In most states, notice of the lien must be filed in a public office within a specified period of time after the completion of the work (usually a few months). Generally, the notice must include the amount claimed, name and address of claimant, description of the work done, and the name of the landowner. There is a statute of limitations for all liens, so that if a creditor does not act on a lien within a certain time period (usually one or two years), the lien is released. The parties may contract to shorten this time period, but not to extend it.

A lien is released when all the work has been completed and the claimant

PROFESSIONAL PUBLICATIONS, INC., P.O. Box 199, San Carlos, CA 94070

has been paid. Because most liens are filed as public record, a release must also be filed with the same office. A lien claimant may also provide periodic waivers of liens for work that has been partially completed and partially paid for.

Foreclosure of a mechanic's lien is handled by the local courts. The judge must first decide if a valid lien exists, a decision which depends on local real estate law and state lien laws. If judgment is for the lien claimant, the property is sold, and proceeds from the sale go to the claimant up to the amount of his claim. Any remainder goes to the debtor.

Because the laws and procedures for filing liens and foreclosures vary in each state, it is important to learn the local ordinances before commencing any work involving the improvement of real property.

B. Real Property Mortgages and other Liens

A real property mortgage is a lien given by the owner of real property to secure the repayment of a loan of money. It differs from a mechanic's lien in that the property is not security for the payment of labor that directly enhances the property, but as security for the payment of a debt. In many cases, the loan is for the purchase of the property, but it need not have any relation to the property at all. Any contractual obligation that can be reduced to a dollar value can be secured by way of a real property mortgage.

Securing a mortgage is procedurally similar to acquiring a mechanic's lien. It must be recorded with the Register of Deed's, and the mortgagor signs a promissory note and mortgage. The mortgage is the lien held by the creditor, giving him the right to claim the property if the loan is not paid. The promissory note makes the mortgagor responsible for the payment of the monetary value of the debt, regardless of what happens to the property. The property cannot be sold without the consent of the person holding the mortgage, who retains claim to the property.

If the mortgage is foreclosed and the property does not bring in enough money to cover the value of the original mortgage, the mortgagor is still responsible for the deficit, and the holder of the note may attach other property belonging to the mortgagor or may garnish his wages.

4. BUSINESS ASSOCIATIONS

Although most people work for others rather than being self-employed, it is not uncommon for the professional engineer to at one time or another consider establishing a consulting practice. In general, there are three types of business ownership: sole proprietorships, partnerships, and corporations. Each form of ownership has its own benefits and disadvantages.

A. Sole Proprietorship

The sole proprietorship is probably the most common. It means the ownership and operation of a business is by an individual. The owner is solely responsible for the operation of the business, even if he hires others to assist him. He is also solely responsible for the debts of the business.

PROFESSIONAL PUBLICATIONS, INC., P.O. Box 199, San Carlos, CA 94070

There is no separation between the property of the business and the owner's personal property. His personal property may be attached to pay the debts of his business. Similarly, all the profits of the business are solely his and he may do with them as he pleases. He need not account to anyone. He may also dissolve the business whenever he pleases, although he will still be personally liable for any debts incurred by his business.

An individual may do business under his own name or under an assumed (fictitious) name. Statutes governing the use of *fictitious names* vary from state to state, but generally require some form of public notice of the name of the business and the real name of the owner. He may also be required to file a statement with the County Clerk and display a copy of this statement at his place of business.

B. Partnerships

A partnership is a business association of two or more persons operating for profit. Each *general partner* shares in the control of the business, the financial profits and losses, and the responsibilities and liabilities of the partnership. A *limited partner* makes a financial investment in a business, but does not share in the operation of the business, and is liable only for the amount of his investment.

Usually, a partnership is established by a contractual agreement. Although not required by law to be in writing, it is rare to enter into a business enterprise without a written contract. Most partnership agreements are fairly detailed and are put in writing for the protection of all partners. The laws governing partnerships are based on the *Uniform Partnership Act,* which has been adopted in its entirety by most states.

A contract establishing a partnership must meet all the requirements of any contract. In particular, it must be voluntary and all parties must be legally competent. The contract should be specific as to the financial investment and liability of each partner, the division of profits and losses, the management obligations of all partners, the accountability of the business's legal and financial dealings, and provisions for the dissolution of the partnership.

The original partnership contract can be amended at any time. If stated in the contract, a partnership interest may be transferred, allowing one partner to sell his interest in the business to another person. However, the original partner is still responsible for his share of the debts outstanding at the time of the transfer. If all parties want to redefine the distribution of duties or financial responsibilities, a new contract should be created.

A partnership is a legal entity and can do business under the assumed name of the partnership -- it can acquire and dispose of real and personal property, and it can sue and be sued. Therefore, a certificate of assumed name must be filed, as with a sole proprietorship. In addition, some states require that a certificate of partnership be filed stating the real names of the partners, along with the name and purpose of the business. These certificates are in addition to the contract between the partners.

All partners have equal rights in managing the business, unless otherwise stated in the partnership agreement. All partners have the right to inspect the financial records or other business documents at any time. Partners do

PROFESSIONAL PUBLICATIONS, INC., P.O. Box 199, San Carlos, CA 94070

not receive a salary for their work; their compensation is a share of the profits as outlined in the partnership contract. The acquisition and disbursement of real property and personal property belonging to the business must be approved by all partners. In some cases, a majority of the partners can manage the firm business even if there is an objecting partner.

The business may be represented by any of the partners. Each partner has the power to bind the other partners (the partnership) when acting within the scope of the business of the partnership. The scope of the partnership business depends upon the nature of the business. For example, a movie theater is not in the business of lending money, so if one partner in a movie theater lends money in the name of the business, without the consent of the other partners, the others will not necessarily be bound by the loan agreement.

Notice given to one partner or knowledge obtained by one partner as to matters relating to the business usually serves to bind the partnership. In other words, all partners need not have actual knowledge; the knowledge of one binds the partnership. It is the responsibility of each partner to keep the others informed.

When a partner is acting within the scope of the partnership business and commits a civil wrong (tort), all of the partners may be held personally liable. The partnership is also liable for the misappropriation of property received by a partner within the scope of the partnership business from a third party (e.g., a partner damages the property of another while that property is being held by the partnership). Partners are personally liable for all debts incurred by the partnership.

Whereas general partners are personally liable for partnership debts which exceed partnership assets, the limited partner has only limited liability. The limited partner invests a certain amount of money in the business, and he is not financially liable for any amount beyond this. His profits are also limited, and are usually specified in the partnership agreement. His participation in the running of the business is limited. Although he has the right to see the financial records in order to protect his own investment, he generally does not get involved in the management of the business. If he does, it could be construed that he is actually acting as a general partner and he could be held liable by creditors.

A partnership exists only as long as the partners choose; it may be dissolved at any time. The partnership dissolves upon the death of a partner or the withdrawal of a partner. The other partners may then create a new partnership agreement, but this will not negate the outstanding obligations of any partner under the terms of the original partnership contract.

C. Corporations

A corporation is a legal entity possessing many of the legal powers of individuals. For example, a corporation may hold title to property and may sue or be sued in its own name. In this way it is like a business partnership.

But unlike a partnership, a corporation exists independently of the people who own and manage it. Its major advantage is, in fact, the separation of management and ownership. The owners of a corporation are shareholders

PROFESSIONAL PUBLICATIONS, INC., P.O. Box 199, San Carlos, CA 94070

whose liabilities extend only to the limits of their financial investments. The corporation is managed by professionals hired by the owners and paid a salary by the corporation.

Another advantage of a corporation is that the life of the corporation does not depend on the continuing participation of specific partners. The ownership of a corporation is easily transferable through stock and does not disrupt the conduct of business. The operation of the corporation is handled by paid employees, and the turnover of staff does not affect the ownership of the corporation.

Private corporations are established by individuals to do business for personal gain. They are also called *stock corporations* because they issue stock to shareholders, who in turn own the corporation, have a right of control over the business, and share in the financial profit. A large number of corporations are owned by the person or persons who established the corporation because they hold a majority of the stock. These are often referred to as *closed corporations* or *closely-held corporations.*

There are also *non-stock corporations,* known as membership corporations, set up as non-profit businesses. Shareholders do not receive financial profit nor do they have any right of control. An example of a membership corporation is a public TV station whose members contribute money, but receive no dividends in return for their investments.

Although primarily regulated by state laws, federal law does play a part in regulating corporations through federal power to regulate interstate activity. Congress has affected the development of corporate enterprises with acts such as the Securities Act of 1933 and the Securites and Exchange Act of 1934, and the establishment of the Securities and Exchange Commission, which is primarily responsible for the overseeing of the sale of corporate stock. Most states have their own statutes regarding the sale of stocks, also known as *blue sky laws,* which are intended to protect investors from fraudulent stock schemes.

The persons forming a stock corporation are known as *incorporators.* The requirements for incorporators vary from state to state, but generally require that all of the incorporators are at least 21 years of age, at least two thirds of them are citizens of the United States, and at least one of them is a resident of the state in which the corporation will exist. In addition, each incorporator must agree to buy at least one share of the corporation's stock.

The *certificate of incorporation* is the document that testifies to the forming of the corporation. It generally includes

- The name of the corporation.

- The names of the incorporators.

- The purpose of the corporation.

- The laws under which it is organized.

- The number and kinds of stock to be issued.

PROFESSIONAL PUBLICATIONS, INC., P.O. Box 199, San Carlos, CA 94070

- The names of the directors.

- The date and state of incorporation.

The certificate is signed and sent to the state authority, usually the secretary of state, and a copy may be filed in the office of the county clerk where the corporation is located.

The shareholders are the owners of the corporation. The specific rights of the shareholders are determined by the *articles of incorporation.* In general, the shareholder has the power of a vote at the annual meeting of shareholders. This vote can determine the direction of the business, but it cannot interfere with the regular business and management policies of the corporation. The shareholder has the right to see the names and numbers of the other shareholders, and he is entitled to see statements of the assets, liabilities, profits, and losses of the corporation. He does not have the right to inspect any other business documents unless he can show reasonable suspicion of wrongful acts. If necessary, a shareholder can sue the corporation for mismanagement of the shareholders' funds.

Although the shareholder is limited in his powers of control, he is protected from financial liability. He can only lose what he has personally invested, and he is not personally responsible for any debts of the corporation.

Corporate activities are confined to those activities stated in the articles of incorporation. Business control of a corporation is in the hands of the Board of Directors, whose powers are prescribed in *by-laws* adopted by the shareholders. The Board of Directors is elected by shareholders; the directors select the personnel who carry on the every day business affairs of the corporation. The board members and corporate officers are paid a salary by the corporation and are not personally liable for any debts incurred by the corporation. They are agents of the corporation, and their actions are binding on the corporation. The directors are responsible for all statements and accountings, and they may be held liable for misrepresentation of facts in reporting the financial position and activities of the corporation.

In many cases, a corporation can be held liable when its officers commit fraudulent acts in the name of the corporation, or if they commit acts outside the scope of corporate authority (also known as *ultra-vires acts* of the corporation). They can also be held liable for damages resulting from negligence.

The board members and officers are not liable for losses due to mistakes in business judgment or to defaults of subordinate employees. The board members and the corporate officers are *fiduciaries,* meaning that they are in positions of trust and confidence with respect to the shareholders, and they must account to the corporation for any secret profits made as a result of their positions. They cannot use their positions within the corporation for personal gain.

If an employee of a corporation, while acting within the scope of the corporate business, commits a civil wrong, the corporation may be held liable. A corporation might itself be fined for committing a crime. A good example of this is when a corporation is found guilty of breaking a ruling of the Environmental Protection Agency or other agency.

PROFESSIONAL PUBLICATIONS, INC., P.O. Box 199, San Carlos, CA 94070

A corporation may be dissolved at the consent of its shareholders or by an act of the legislature that created it. Some corporations are only established for specific periods of time, at the ends of which they are dissolved. If a corporation becomes insolvent, it may be dissolved by judicial proceedings. A corporation may be merged into another corporation, or it may be reorganized such that it is, in effect, a different enterprise.

D. Other Associations

There are a number of organizations that exist in the business world. Labor unions and unincorporated civic organizations are examples of these types of organizations. They exist by common agreement of a group of people. The liability of such groups is ordinarily limited to the individual liability of a person belonging to the group. For the most part, these business organizations are not legal entities and do not have a separate life outside of the persons involved.

In dealing with any business organization or group, one should be sure that he is dealing with authorized agents of the association. Otherwise, any contract made may not be binding. It may be necessary to read the articles of incorporation or partnership agreement to make sure that a contract is properly executed. The person signing the contract should have the power to bind the business entity and his title should ordinarily be included in the contract.

5. AGENCY

Agency is a legally created relationship. In general, whatever one may lawfully do for himself may be delegated to an agent by means of an agency contract. An *agent* deals with a third party on behalf of his *principal,* the party from whom the agent's powers are derived. The acts of the agent have the same legal effect as if they were done by the principal.

The agent/principal relationship is created by contract, either express or implied. The principal is bound by the acts of his agent, although the extent of the agent's powers varies depending on the type of relationship created. A real estate agent, for example, is empowered only to negotiate the sale of real estate. Most professional entertainers hire agents to negotiate employment contracts. Salesmen are usually agents of their companies and have the power to negotiate sales on behalf of the company. Agents have *fiduciary responsibility* towards their principals, meaning that agents are bound to be loyal and honest. If an agent is devious against his principal, the agent will be personally liable for his actions.

Any person who is legally competent to enter into contractual relationships is eligible to be an agent or a principal. A minor may be an agent, and his acts will bind the principal, but as a minor he may avoid his own contractual obligations. Corporations may act as agents or principals if such action does not conflict with their by-laws.

An agent's powers are expressed in his contract, but other powers may be implied as needed for the agent to carry out his responsibilities. As with any contract, the terms should be as unambiguous as possible, or questions about the liability of either the agent or principal might become an issue.

PROFESSIONAL PUBLICATIONS, INC., P.O. Box 199, San Carlos, CA 94070

The principal is bound by the acts of his agent if those acts are committed within the scope of the agency contract.

The principal must compensate the agent for his services. Otherwise, no contract exists and anything the agent does for the principal becomes a favor and is not legally binding.

The liability of both the principal and the agent is defined by the contract. The agent/principal relationship also carries implied liability for each party. In the most general sense, the agent is implicitly bound to obey the instructions of his principal, be loyal and trustworthy, keep confidential information, have no conflict of interests, and execute his duties with skill and due care. The principal is not only legally bound to uphold the agency contract, and accept the acts of the agent as expressed in the contract, but he is also liable for injuries to the agent in the line of duty.

If an agent creates a contract with a third party who has the expressed knowledge that the agent is representing someone else, the agent has no liability for the performance of the contract. If he does not disclose that he is an agent for someone else, or is acting outside the express or implied authority of his agency, then he is held personally liable.

If the third party is not aware that the agent is representing someone else, he has the choice of holding either the principal or the agent liable. This is only applicable if the third party had no way of knowing that the agent was negotiating on behalf of someone else. If he did know this, he could only sue the principal.

The third party is bound to the principal according to any contract created with an agent, even if the principal is undisclosed, as long as the agent was acting within the scope of his authority. The third party is not liable to the agent, except in a possible tort against the agent.

If the agent commits a civil wrong, the third party may sue the agent individually or he may sue the agent and principal jointly. This only applies to wrongs committed within the scope of his actual or implied authority as agent. The principal is held liable for any damages resulting from the acts of his agent.

A *power of attorney* is a written form of agency contract by which you can make another person your agent for any or all business transactions. A *general power of attorney* enables the agent to conduct any business that you could do yourself. A *special power of attorney* enables the agent to act in your behalf only in a specific situation.

6. SALES

The sale of an item is such a common experience that most people do not consider it a contractual obligation, unless the item is of substantial cost. However, every sale or purchase involves the creation and execution of an implicit sales contract.

PROFESSIONAL PUBLICATIONS, INC., P.O. Box 199, San Carlos, CA 94070

A. Definition

A *sale* consists of the passing of title for an item from the seller to the buyer for a price. A *cash sale* is the simultaneous exchange of goods for a price. A *conditional sale* is a sale based upon the condition that the seller will pay the full price in the future, usually paid in periodic installments. In this latter case, the seller keeps the title, but the buyer gains possession of the goods, and assumes all risk. Regardless of what happens to the goods, he is liable to the seller for the full price.

The contract is between a seller, or the vendor, and a buyer, the vendee. The seller agrees to transfer the goods to the buyer for a price. It is a mutual exchange of consideration. A sales contract may be absolute or conditional. Any form of sales agreement that meets the requisites for a valid contract is legal.

There is a difference between a contract to sell and a contract of sale. A *contract to sell* is a promise to transfer ownership of specific goods some-time in the future, when those goods become available. Only when actual ownership is transferred and payment is made is there a *contract of sale*. For example, a buyer might contract with a company to buy a set of ency-clopedias, receiving and paying for a single book each month. The contract to sell is the agreement to buy the complete set one at a time. Each month, a contract of sale is executed as each separate book is delivered and paid for.

Contracts of sale come under the statute of frauds, which states that the sale of items of substantial value (usually over $500) must be in writing. In many cases, if the sale falls under the statute of frauds, but the contract is not in writing, it might still be enforceable if the buyer has taken pos-session of the items.

For the most part, sales contracts are administered by state law, except when interstate commerce is involved, in which case federal law prevails. The *Uniform Commercial Code* is a set of guidelines developed by govern-ment agents and business advisors for the creation of laws governing commercial law. It has been adopted by most states. It describes in detail how sales contracts should be negotiated and executed, and deter-mines when title passes, who bears the risks, and other aspects of sales transactions when the parties have not expressly agreed on the particular point involved.

B. Title

Title to property is what defines the ownership of the item. Regardless of who has possession of it, legal ownership is defined by the title. In gen-eral, the seller cannot transfer title that he does not possess himself. How-ever, there are some exceptions to this.

- If someone were falsely led to believe that he had title to something and then sold it, the sale would be legal. This is the *principle of estoppel,* which states that if a person, by his prior attitude, led someone to believe something and act in reliance upon it, that implied behavior will be upheld in court.

- If an agent sells goods for his principal, title passes, even though the agent has no title to the goods himself.

- If a person purchases a promissory note payable to the bearer before maturity, he is an innocent purchaser and acquires a good title to the note even though the person selling it did not have legal title because the note had not yet reached maturity.

Exactly when the title actually passes from seller to buyer is of importance, because the risk of loss is generally with the person who has the title. If the timing is explicitly stated in the sales contract, then title passes as agreed by the parties. If it is not expressed in the contract, then title passes when the goods are delivered. Because of the risks usually involved in delivery, and the reliance in many instances on commercial carriers, it is important to specify in a sales agreement when the buyer receives title.

C. Conditions and Warranties

A *condition* in a sales contract is a stipulation, either express or implied, that must be performed before the title of the goods can pass from seller to buyer. If this stipulation is not met, the contract is considered breached. The injured party, however, has the right to waive the condition and discharge the contract.

A *warranty* is a guarantee by the seller that the goods meet certain requirements. It is separate from the sales contract, but dependent on it. There can be no recovery for breach of warranty if there is no binding sales contract. A warranty and a *guarantee* are the same thing; they are statements guaranteeing the product against defects, and usually include an agreement to repair or replace the item within a certain period of time if found to be defective.

A warranty can be either express or implied. An *express warranty* is in writing and states very specifically what the warranty covers. An *implied warranty* is implied by law and guarantees that the seller has the right to sell it and that it is of reasonable quality and suited to the function for which it is sold. Because this is open to interpretation, federal law requires consumer products to be sold with specific terms of guarantee.

The most important and uncontestable element of the implied warranty is that the seller has the right to sell the goods in question. He must have the title in his possession. This implies that the buyer will be able to take possession of the goods with no contest, that the goods are free of encumbrances by third parties, and that no other party has any claim on the goods.

Implied warranty also means that the seller guarantees that the goods are of reasonable quality, at least to the point of being fit to fulfill the jobs that they are claimed to be able to do. When the buyer makes known to the seller the purpose for which the item is desired and it appears that the buyer has relied on the seller's skill or judgment, there is an implied warranty that the item will be reasonably suitable for that purpose. If the buyer did not make known the use for which he desired the item, the seller cannot be held responsible for its suitability.

If the buyer inspects the goods before accepting, there is no implied warranty against defects that could be detected by such inspection. If he is given an opportunity to inspect the goods and declines, he waives his right to recover damages. If an article is sold by trademark or tradename, there is no implied warranty that the article is suitable for any particular purpose, since the buyer does not rely on the seller's skill or judgment. In such a case, the manufacturer may be held liable for the suitability of the product for its stated purposes.

An express warranty is a statement made by a seller at the time of the sale that guarantees the title, character, or quality of the goods. If this warranty is breached, the injured party has the right to claim damages, but it does not void the sales contract.

An express warranty is created when products are sold by description. *Sales by description* are sales in which the buyer describes the product he wants by function or specification. For example, he might ask for a particular model number or the seller might describe an unseen product in very specific terms. This constitutes an express warranty that the product he received will correspond with the description supplied. For example, Smith ordered some lumber from Brown who said that it was "top quality." When Smith received it, he discovered that it was of very low quality. The goods did not meet the description made by the seller, so Smith could justifiably refuse the shipment.

In a *sale by sample,* the buyer has bought goods by bulk based on a small sample of the item. This creates an express warranty that all the items in the bulk will correspond to the sample. The buyer has the right to inspect and compare the goods with the sample. By supplying the sample for inspection, the seller (or manufacturer) is guaranteeing that such an inspection is sufficient to determine the quality of the items and that all items in the order will be of equal quality.

A warranty can expressly state what is not covered by the warranty. If this is part of the sales contract, the buyer can make no claims against defects or suitability. This is a *warranty disclaimer.* For example, Smith bought some paint. The warranty explicitly stated that it was not guaranteed for outdoor use. When Smith used it to paint the outside of his house and it peeled off in two weeks, he could not sue the paint company for a defective product.

If a product is found to be defective, damages can be claimed to the limit of the warranty. The defendant must be able to prove that the defect was not apparent and that the product was being used properly. If the product has caused sickness or injury, the manufacturer is generally held liable for the cost of the illness or injury.

D. Rights of Seller and Buyer

Usually the problems that arise from a sales contract are the result of the failure to deliver goods or the refusal to accept goods, or the destruction or damage of the goods before delivery. Once a sales contract is established, it is the contractual duty of the seller to deliver the goods according to the terms of the contract. If the seller meets the terms, it is the contractual duty of the buyer to accept the goods and pay for them. Unless stated otherwise, delivery and payment are concurrent conditions.

If the buyer refuses to accept the goods when delivered, and the goods are

PROFESSIONAL PUBLICATIONS, INC., P.O. Box 199, San Carlos, CA 94070

not damaged and meet the requirements of the contract, the seller may sue for breach of contract. Generally he will recover the damages resulting from the breach. For example, Smith agreed to sell Brown 1,000 resistors for 8 cents each, but Brown refused to accept them, forcing Smith to sell them to someone else for 6 cents each. He sued Brown for breach of contract and recovered the difference in sale price between the original contract price and what Smith was able to get from someone else.

If the seller has not been paid, but has delivered the goods and title has passed to the buyer, he may sue for breach of contract. So in the above example, if Brown had accepted the shipment, he would have title to the goods. If he did not pay for them, Smith would be able to sue him for the total price of the goods.

When the seller has not been paid, but title has passed to the buyer, the seller has several courses of action.

- If the goods are still in the seller's possession, the seller has a *seller's lien* on the goods or a right to retain the goods. Even if the goods have been shipped, the seller has a seller's lien and he can recover the goods in transit, or within 10 days of shipment.

- If the buyer becomes insolvent, the seller has the right to recover possession of the goods.

- If the seller still has possession of the goods, he has the right to resell them.

- The seller may rescind the sales contract.

If the wrong quantity of goods is delivered, the buyer may choose to accept or reject the shipment, or he may accept only the portion for which he contracted to buy. If the goods are delivered by the seller to a common carrier, (that is, train, rail express, etc.), it is usually considered delivery to the buyer unless specified differently by the contract.

If the vendor fails to deliver the goods or damages them in any way so that they are no longer useful for the purpose the buyer intended them for, the buyer may sue for breach of contract. If the title has passed to the buyer, but he has not received the goods, he may sue for *specific performance.* That is, he may sue for the goods.

E. Terms of Delivery

The delivery of goods is an important part of a sales transaction. Because there is often a time period after the goods have left the seller and before they reach the buyer, it is important to understand the more common terms of delivery. The type of delivery agreed on determines when title passes.

- C.O.D. -- Cash on Delivery. The buyer pays cash for the merchandise when it is delivered.

- F.O.B. -- Free on Board. This type of sales transaction requires the seller to deliver the goods to a designated place. This is usually a commercial carrier, but could be either the buyer's or

PROFESSIONAL PUBLICATIONS, INC., P.O. Box 199, San Carlos, CA 94070

seller's place of business. When delivery is made, the buyer assumes title.

- F.A.S. -- Free Alongside Ship. This means that the goods must be delivered to a specific place to be loaded onto a ship. Title remains with the seller until the goods have been delivered on the dock or alongside the ship. This differs from F.O.B. in which the seller has the risk until the goods are on board the ship.

- C.I.F. -- Cost, Insurance, and Freight. This is a requirement that the seller pay for the insurance and freight of the goods until they reach the destination. The buyer assumes the risk of loss during shipment.

- C. & F. -- Cost and Freight. This is like C.I.F. except that the risk during shipment is with the seller.

- E.S. -- Ex. Ship. This terms means literally "out of the ship." It means that the title passes to the buyer when the goods are taken off the ship.

7. TORT

A *tort* is a civil wrong committed against a person or his property, business, emotional well-being, or reputation that causes damage. It is a breach of the rights of an individual to be secure in his person and property and be free from undue harrassment. For an invasion of personal rights to be a tort and a valid cause for legal action, there must be resulting damages.

The difference between a tort and a crime, in a very general sense, is that a crime is a wrong against society, something that threatens the peace and safety of the community. A *criminal lawsuit* is then brought by the state against a defendant. A crime may also be a tort in that it results in personal damages. The victim of the crime may also bring a tort suit against the defendant to recover damages.

Tort law is primarily state law, and is predominantly case law rather than statutory. The decision in a tort case is based on three conditions:

- If a person's rights have been infringed upon.

- If it was a result of negligence or actual intent on the part of the plaintiff.

- If the defendant suffered damages as a direct result.

Tort law is concerned with compensation, not punishment. Compensation is usually a certain sum of money. The amount of the judgment stems directly from the amount of damage suffered as a direct result of the tort. Nominal damages may be awarded to the plaintiff as justification for the wrong suffered in cases where the actual damages do not warrant a substantial award. Special damages may be awarded if the defendant suffered other losses as a result of the original damage. Other types of damages may be

PROFESSIONAL PUBLICATIONS, INC., P.O. Box 199, San Carlos, CA 94070

awarded in special cases. For example, if the tort was the result of malicious intent, punitive damages may be awarded. But the damages in a tort case are primarily meant to be compensatory.

A. Misrepresentation

Misrepresentation is a false statement by a person of a material fact that he knows to be false, with the intent to deceive another person. If that person then relies on this information and acts on it in such a way as to cause damages to himself, he can claim damages in a tort case.

Most commonly, misrepresentation is a factor in a breach of contract suit, but such a wrong can be treated as either a tort or a breach of contract, depending on the type of damages requested by the defendant. For example, if you bought a car and it was stated in the contract that it had recently had a brake job and that the brakes were therefore in top condition, and you had an accident due to brake failure, you could sue for breach of contract or for personal injury in a tort case.

Sometimes, misrepresentation does not involve a contractual agreement, and is therefore clearly a tort. In these cases, the reliance of the plaintiff on the misrepresented facts must be proven beyond a reasonable doubt and there must be an intent to deceive on the part of the defendant. Merely bragging or teasing does not constitute misrepresentation.

B. Nuisance

Nuisance is a type of tort that involves the annoyance or disturbance of a person in the possession of his property, such that the ordinary use or occupation of the property becomes physically uncomfortable. The tort of nuisance is a violation of a person's right to safety, comfort, and the enjoyment of his own property.

The defendant must be using his property unlawfully or unreasonably and consequently damage the other person's use of his property or create a threat of damage. For example, if one person were to have a faulty air conditioning unit that made enough noise to disturb the neighbors, it would constitute a nuisance. In cases like this, judgment is usually for the removal of the nuisance, unless actual damages have been incurred. In some cases, merely the threat of damages is enough for a tort action. For example, the threat to your children's safety because of toxic waste being dumped by a neighboring factory constitutes a tort.

Nuisances may be public or private, depending upon whether they affect the community or only an individual. If there is a *public nuisance,* action may be brought by the group of people affected. Action may also be brought when there is a potential for a nuisance tort. For example, if there were dangerous chemicals lying about on some property such that children or animals might be endangered by them, the owner of the property could be sued. However, since no actual damages had been suffered, the judgment would simply be the requirement that the owner remove or safely guard the chemicals.

C. Negligence

Negligence is not using proper care in a situation, resulting in damages to

PROFESSIONAL PUBLICATIONS, INC., P.O. Box 199, San Carlos, CA 94070

property or injury to persons. Proper care and safety can be a very subjective judgment, but in general terms it is that diligence exercised by a reasonably prudent person. Any damages suffered as the result of another's negligence can be compensated for in a tort case.

A tort of negligence requires three things:

- The plaintiff must have a duty to the defendant to provide safety.

- This duty must have been neglected by the defendant.

- The plaintiff must have suffered damages as a result.

The negligence must be the direct cause of the damages. However, merely proving negligence on the part of the defendant is not always sufficient to recover damages, because the defendant has several options that he can exercise as a defense. The most common of these is *contributory negligence.* This is where the defendant proves that the plaintiff was equally as negligent, or might have prevented the damages if the plaintiff had taken due care.

In some cases, the defendant can prove that the plaintiff willingly took a risk that was not necessary and that he was aware of, thereby absolving the defendant of responsibility for any damages suffered. For example, if a person were to climb a scaffolding after being warned that it was dangerous, he could not sue for damages if he fell and suffered injuries. He has voluntarily assumed the risk, and thus no one else can be held liable.

One area in which personal injury liability has been heavily regulated by state and federal statutes is *workmen's compensation.* These laws are designed to provide equitable compensation for a person who is injured in the course of his job. Most employers are required to carry insurance to protect them from the claims of employees that have been injured. This protects the employer and also ensures that the employee will receive compensation. The amount received depends on the actual cost of medical expenses, the amount of the plaintiff's wages, the nature and extent of his injuries, the length of his disability, and the number of dependents.

D. Bailments

A *bailment* is the delivery of goods or personal property by one person to another for a specific purpose. The person receiving the goods, known as the *bailee,* does not gain title to the property. He only has temporary possession of it, and is absolutely liable for damages or misdelivery of the goods. Most commonly, a bailment is assumed when an item is left with someone for repair.

Bailments fall under the category of torts because they have to do with the protection of personal property. There are three types of bailments:

- Bailment for the benefit of both bailor and bailee.

- Bailment for the sole benefit of bailor.

- Bailment for the sole benefit of bailee.

PROFESSIONAL PUBLICATIONS, INC., P.O. Box 199, San Carlos, CA 94070

A bailment is for the benefit of both bailor and bailee if the bailee receives some property belonging to the bailor for a purpose that is advantageous to them both. For example, one person leaves something in the possession of another for repair or servicing and agrees to pay him for the service. The bailee is responsible for safeguarding the property while it is in his possession, and the bailor is obligated to pay him for the services when the property is returned.

In a bailment for the sole benefit of the bailor, the bailee gets no compensation for the services he provides to the bailor. He has merely promised to do something for the bailor. There is no enforceable contract between them because there is no compensation, but as soon as he takes possession of the bailor's property, he is responsible for it, and if he does not return it in a suitable condition, the bailor can sue him for damages. For example, Smith offers to fix a piece of equipment for Brown. Brown is not going to pay him for the repair, but as long as Smith has the equipment in his possession, he is responsible for it. If he does not return it, or if it becomes damaged, Brown can sue for its return or repair.

A bailment for the sole benefit of the bailee is one in which the bailor gives the bailee some goods for his temporary use and expects only to receive the goods back in the same condition. In other words, the bailee borrows something from the bailor. If he damages the property while it is in his possession, the bailor may sue him for damages.

8. NEGOTIABLE INSTRUMENTS

A *negotiable instrument* is a type of contract devised to facilitate commercial transactions. It is a written document that conforms to certain legal rules and can be negotiated (that is, transferred) from one party to another as a means of exchange or credit in place of money. It is transferable through endorsement and delivery or simply through delivery. It states very simply that the person in possession of it is entitled to a certain sum of money from a particular source. Any person who receives a negotiable instrument can collect the face value of it on demand.

The three most common forms of negotiable instruments are:

- Promissory note.
- Bill of exchange.
- Bank check.

The *maker,* or *drawer,* is the person or business promising to pay the money. The *drawee* is the person or business (a bank, for example) who actually has the money. The payee is the person who is to receive the money.

Other forms of exchange are possible, but they may not be negotiable as defined by law. If the instrument is not negotiable, the holder is subject to all claims against the instrument by third parties or prior holders.

PROFESSIONAL PUBLICATIONS, INC., P.O. Box 199, San Carlos, CA 94070

A. Negotiability

To be *negotiable,* the instrument must possess the following properties:

- It must be in writing.

- It must be properly signed by the maker or drawer.

- It must contain an unconditional promise or order to pay by the drawer. These are the words of negotiability, and include such phrases as "Pay to the order of..." or "Pay to bearer". An instrument reading "Pay to the order of Smith if...." is not negotiable, because there is a condition attached to the payment.

- It must be payable in money only, not goods or services, and the amount must be a definite sum.

- The payment must be made to the order of some designated person or to the holder of the document.

- The money is to be paid on demand or at a designated time, such as a calendar date, or upon the occurrence of something that is sure to happen. This is the *date of maturity.* The payment cannot depend on an occurrence that might not happen, or it becomes a conditional term of payment. For example, if payment is to be made upon the death of Smith, it is a certainty, whereas if payment were to be made upon Smith's 21st birthday, it would be conditional, because Smith could die before reaching 21.

B. Promissory Notes

A *promissory note* is an unconditional written promise by one or more parties to pay to the bearer or to another person a certain sum of money at a specified time. The party who makes the promise is called the *maker* or *promisor,* and the party to whom the promise is made is called the *payee* or *promisee.*

The note can be in any form as long as it meets the requirements of negotiability. It may contain additional information, such as an agreed upon interest rate, or a schedule of payment. It might also include the place where the note is to be presented for payment.

If the payee wishes to receive the money before the due date of the note, he may transfer the note to another person by endorsing it in the name of that person. That is, he writes "Pay to the order of ..." and signs it. The third party pays him the amount of the note and becomes holder of the note. On the due date, the holder presents the note to the maker for payment.

The note is discharged by payment and the maker may ask that the note be surrendered to him at that time to prevent it from being transferred to another person who might then have legal right to demand payment. If the maker does not pay the specified sum on the due date, it is considered a breach of contract, and the holder of the note can sue him for full payment.

PROFESSIONAL PUBLICATIONS, INC., P.O. Box 199, San Carlos, CA 94070

C. Bills of Exchange

A *bill of exchange* (or *draft*) is an unconditional written order from one person, the drawer, to another, the drawee, to pay a third person, the payee, a certain sum of money at a specified time. The order is based on some relationship between the drawer and the drawee, such as a business partnership or a bank account. A *foreign bill of exchange* is drawn in one country or state for payment in another country or state. If drawn for payment in the state where drawn, the bill is an *inland bill of exchange.*

The date on which payment is due to the third party must be clearly stated on the draft, but may be indicated as "at sight." This is a *sight draft,* which is payable at the time the payee presents it to the drawer.

A *time draft* is one that has a specific date of maturity; the payment is due on a specific date or a specific amount of time after the draft is presented for payment. It may be stated as due "at 30 days sight," which means 30 days after presented to the drawee. He accepts it by dating and signing it. It is now negotiable and may be transferred to another holder who will then be entitled to payment when the 30 days have elapsed.

However, the drawee may refuse to accept the draft. He has no obligation to the payee; his obligations are to the drawer, determined by their relationship. The drawee is accountable only to the drawer; the payee cannot sue the drawee for payment. Only the drawer is liable to either party.

D. Checks

The negotiable instrument most people are familiar with is the bank check, a written document that authorizes a bank to pay a certain sum of money to the person named on the check. The bank is the drawee, the person holding the check is the payee, and the person writing and signing the check is the drawer. It is a type of bill of exchange, and its use follows the same pattern.

The bank may refuse to pay the money if there are insufficient funds in the drawer's account to cover the check. The drawer is then responsible to the payee -- the bank has no responsibility to the payee. The bank is liable to the drawer if it does not honor a check for which there are funds.

9. REAL PROPERTY LAW

Real property is land and buildings. It can also include things that are an inherent part of the land, such as minerals and water. Trees and other growth are part of real property, but a growing crop is considered personal property because it is easily removed and is intended for separate sale.

Real property law is primarily state law. Unlike contract law or tort law, real property law has evolved very differently in different parts of the country. Although property law was at one time concerned primarily with title of ownership and conveyance of that title from seller to buyer, it now encompasses land use, through land planning agencies, zoning ordinances in urban areas, and environmental protection concerns.

PROFESSIONAL PUBLICATIONS, INC., P.O. Box 199, San Carlos, CA 94070

A. Title: Warranty and Quitclaim Deeds

Ownership of real property is determined by possession of the title. When real property is sold, title is passed from seller to buyer by way of a deed. A *deed* is a written instrument, also called a *conveyance,* by which a landowner transfers the ownership of his land.

The legality of the deed and the process by which a deed is executed is determined by state law. The essential elements of a deed are:

- A grantor. The person conveying the property must be of legal age and of sound mind.

- A grantee. Without a grantee, a deed is void.

- Proof of consideration. Consideration of a deed is usually the price of the property.

- Words of conveyance. These are usually words like "convey and warrant", "grant", "bargain", or "sell".

- Description of property.

- Signature and seal of grantor. A signature is essential; some states also require a seal.

- The delivery of the completed deed to the grantee.

The deed may also include:

- Warranties of title.

- List of mortgages and other encumbrances.

- Date of the deed.

- Witnesses.

- Acknowledgment, notarization.

- Revenue stamps, if required by state law.

Every deed contains a description of the land, which includes a detailed delineation of the boundaries of the land. Boundaries are described by a land surveyor who creates the legal description, which may be one of two types. A *metes and bounds description* consists of measurements and descriptions of natural boundaries, such as streets or streams. *Government surveys* consist of precise lines of demarcation, running east-west and north-south, creating rectangular tracts of land that can be referenced in a *grid (township) description.*

A deed is always filed in a public office, usually the Registrar of Deeds. The two types of deeds most commonly used are warranty deeds and quitclaim deeds.

Warranty Deeds. A *warranty deed* is a conveyance of title that contains

PROFESSIONAL PUBLICATIONS, INC., P.O. Box 199, San Carlos, CA 94070

certain guarantees. Primarily, it guarantees that the deed conveys a good and unencumbered title, which means that the grantor of the deed has a good title and that no one else has claim to the property. It is also a guarantee that the person receiving the property will not be evicted by someone having a better title to the property.

If any of the requirements for a warranty deed are not met, the grantee may sue the grantor for damages. This includes cases where the grantor does not own the complete title or where someone else holds a mortgage on the property.

Quitclaim Deeds. A *quitclaim deed* conveys only the grantor's present interest in the land, not the land itself. The deed does not guarantee anything -- it does not guarantee that the grantor has any interest in the land at all. If the grantor acquires interest in the land after the quitclaim deed is executed, he retains it. The grantor cannot be sued for damages incurred by the grantee.

B. Adverse Possession

In some cases, a good title may be overruled by another person who takes possession of the land and puts it to good use. This is the principle of *adverse possession.* It means that if a person has taken possession of a piece of property without permission of the owner, he will be able to acquire a good title to the land if his possession of the land meets certain requirements. Even the holder of the original title cannot evict him.

This ruling serves two main purposes. First, it encourages the use of the land. For example, if a landowner lives in another state, and his land is lying fallow, someone could take possession of the land and put it to good use. The person using the land is entitled to own it. Secondly, the real title to a piece of property might not be discoverable. In many cases, a title depends on a series of old transactions that are difficult to trace, and the legal owner is deceased or otherwise unavailable. A person may take possession of the land to acquire the title.

For adverse possession to lead to a legal title, it must meet certain requirements. The dispossessing occupant must be in actual possession of the land, utilizing it in some way. He must make it known that he is denying the owner's claim of title. His possession must be known to the owner and must be continuous. The time period for adverse possesion to take effect varies, but is in the order of 15-20 years.

C. Easements

An *easement* is a right by one landowner to use a piece of land owned by another for a special purpose. The most common form of easement is created mainly for the benefit of one tract of land, so an easement always involves two tracts of land owned by different persons. For example, Smith and Jones own two adjoining pieces of property. Smith gives Jones the right to cross Smith's property from a highway to Jones' property. Jones has an easement on Smith's property. An easement usually remains with the land, so if Jones sells his property to Brown, Brown will retain the easement to Smith's property.

An easement is usually created by a written agreement. An *express grant of*

PROFESSIONAL PUBLICATIONS, INC., P.O. Box 199, San Carlos, CA 94070

easement should contain all the requirements of a formal deed and may in some cases be incorporated into a deed. Easements may also be created by a contract. *Implied easements* are created under certain circumstances. For example, if two pieces of property are originally owned by one person who sells one piece to another person, the original owner can retain an easement on the piece of sold property if he had been using that property for a necessary purpose. An easement may also be created by *prescription*, which is similar to acquiring a title by adverse possession.

D. Zoning

Zoning is the allocation of areas of a city made by city planners to regulate the use of land. The intent of zoning ordinances is to protect public health and safety. The right of individuals to do what they want with their property is overridden for the sake of the community. Zoning ordinances lead to uncongested population, enable public transportation to function smoothly, secure safe and quiet residential areas, and enable public services, such as police, fire, and sanitation, to protect the community.

Zoning ordinances designate a particular area as either residential, commercial, or manufacturing. Up until recently, residences have been allowed in commercial zones, and any type of use could be made of manufacturing zones. But ordinances are moving toward more exclusive restrictions on land use. Zoning ordinances can always be contested in municipal court if they are considered unreasonable in light of valid needs. The needs of a city are constantly changing, and as usable land becomes scarcer, it becomes more important to make wise use of the available land.

Many factors are taken into consideration when zoning an individual piece of land. The use being made of surrounding areas has a direct bearing. It would be unreasonable to locate a residential area right next to an industrial area. However, there will always be, by necessity, an arbitrary line dividing zones so it is not possible to avoid placing different zones next to each other. Zoning ordinances will allow, within reason, land to be used for activities incidental to the zoned use of it. For example, a food store might be allowed in an apartment within an area not zoned for commercial use.

Many times a zoning ordinance will include restrictions on the size and shapes of buildings that can be erected. This is to control the density of buildings in the area. For example, some residential areas require buildings to be a certain distance from the street or limit the height of multi-story buildings. An ordinance can also specify a minimum size of lots in a particular area.

As needs change, zoning ordinances are revised. Areas that were once residential may be rezoned commercial as use of the land changes and surrounding areas expand. In many cases, where the area is not being rezoned, but restrictions are changing, a building that met the requirements at the time it was built will not suddenly be considered a violation. And often, the city will allow a use to be made of land against current zoning ordinances if just cause of hardship can be shown or if the ordinance allows special exceptions.

PROFESSIONAL PUBLICATIONS, INC., P.O. Box 199, San Carlos, CA 94070

E. Leases, Landlords, and Tenants

A *lease* is a contract defining a relationship between the landlord and the tenant, and the rights and responsibilities of each. It is also a conveyance by the landlord to the tenant of the right to occupy the land for a specified period of time. Most leases fix a definite uniform rent to be paid for the duration of the lease, whereas some, usually long-term leases, specify a gradually increasing rate of rent. Whatever the requirements of the lease, it should be stated explicitly as with any contract.

There are some requirements that must be met by a lease in order to be binding. In most states, a lease for less than a year may be verbal, but a lease for a period over a year must be in writing. Many states require that a lease meet the requirements of a deed. The landowner, also known as the lessor, must be of legal age and of sound mind. The tenant, or lessor, must also be of age and of sound mind. The lease must contain a specific description of the property to be leased, and must specify the duration of the lease, the rent, and the manner in which the rent is to be paid. It must be signed by both the lessor and the lessee. Some states require a seal, notarization, acknowledgment, or recording. In all cases, the lease must be delivered to the lessee by the lessor.

The lease usually specifies what uses the tenant may make of the property. If not specified, the tenant is free to use the property in any lawful manner. It should also be very explicit as to what the tenant is expected to provide in the way of utilities and repairs. Many states have statutes that require the landlord to keep the property in safe condition and if the tenant or a guest is injured as the result of a dangerous condition, such as a faulty staircase, the landlord may be held liable.

The tenant is not required to make any repairs unless he was directly responsible for the damage. It is his duty, however, to take reasonable precautions to prevent damages to the property if possible. He may not make any structural changes to the property without permission of the landlord. Under a lease for a business property, the tenant is usually required to make ordinary repairs, while the landlord is responsible for all major and unusual repairs.

A lease is terminated when the specified period of time has elapsed or by agreement between the lessor and the lessee. In most instances, the tenant must give notice (usually 30 days) to the landlord that he intends to vacate the property. Otherwise, he could be held liable for the rent. A tenant can be evicted by the landlord for failure to live up to the terms of the lease, either by not paying rent as agreed or for using the property for a purpose explicitly not allowed by the lease.

F. Lateral Support

Owners of adjacent pieces of property are liable to one another to provide adequate protection of each other's property. They have the right to the support of the land in its "natural condition." That is, whatever support is provided by the soil, untouched by man, to buildings built on the land cannot be taken away by one owner to the detriment of the other owner without adequate compensation. Primarily, this means that if one owner begins to excavate near the property line, he may be held liable for damages to the adjoining property as a result of the excavation.

PROFESSIONAL PUBLICATIONS, INC., P.O. Box 199, San Carlos, CA 94070

The excavator must give notice (usually 10 days) to the owner of the adjoining property. Both the excavator and the adjoining owner have the right to go upon each other's property when necessary to build additional support for existing buildings. The excavator may be liable to damages if

- He did not notify his neighbor of the excavation.

- The actual excavation was different from that described in the notice.

- The excavation is left open for a long period of time.

- The excavation could have been accomplished safely by using other methods.

- The excavation fills with water and damage is caused by water seepage.

For example, Smith and Jones own adjacent tracts of land. Smith has a building that is only a few feet from the dividing line between their property. Jones wants to do excavation near the line in order to construct a building on his property. If soil from Smith's property collapses into the excavation, Jones may be held liable for any resulting damages to Smith's building. However, Smith cannot expect Jones' soil to provide support to his building, so if Jones excavates with due care, and Smith's building collapses due to the weight of the building, Jones is not liable. However, Jones is responsible for notifying Smith of his intentions to excavate so that Jones may take precautions to protect his building.

G. Fixtures

A *fixture* is a piece of personal property that has been attached to land or buildings such that it can be considered permanent. It is, by law, a part of the real property. For example, a kitchen sink is personal property until it is installed, at which time it becomes a part of the real property.

When real property is sold, all fixtures go to the buyer, even though they might not be explicitly mentioned in the deed. It is often a point of controversy whether an item is a fixture or a piece of personal property. Determination is based on the following:

- If the article is attached to a building in such a way that its removal would damage the buildings, it is considered a fixture. This includes such things as plumbing fixtures or permanently affixed floor coverings.

- If an article was constructed especially for a particular building and is necessary to carry out the purpose for which the building was constructed, it is considered a fixture. An example of this is special machinery designed for an industrial plant.

- In some cases, the deciding factor is the intention of the party installing the article. If it might be reasonably construed that the person intended the item to be permanent, it is considered a fixture. A common example is the kitchen stove or refrigerator

PROFESSIONAL PUBLICATIONS, INC., P.O. Box 199, San Carlos, CA 94070

installed in an apartment house.

- It also sometimes matters if the land is being sold or rented. Generally, if land is being sold, most items that might be considered permanent are sold as part of the property. However, most items installed on property by a tenant are not considered fixtures and may be removed by the tenant. They do not attach to the property.

Some fixtures may be removed by a tenant if the tenant had purchased and installed them himself. These include:

- Trade fixtures are items necessary to a businessman's trade and are installed in a leased building so as to enable him to conduct business. Examples are restaurant equipment and beauty shop fixtures.

- Agricultural fixtures are installed by a tenant farmer so that he may farm the land. These includes tool sheds, hen houses, and bee hives.

- Any article installed by a tenant for his own comfort are considered domestic and ornamental fixtures and may be removed by the tenant. This includes such things as window blinds, carpeting, and shelving.

PROFESSIONAL PUBLICATIONS, INC., P.O. Box 199, San Carlos, CA 94070

REVIEW PROBLEMS FOR PART I

In Problems 1-4, are the written instruments negotiable? Give reasons in each case.

1. City, State, November 10, 19xx.
   Due John Smith, one hundred and fifty dollars
   ($150).
   Value received.

   George Brown (signature)

2. City, State, November 10, 19xx.
   Six months after date I promise to pay John Smith
   the sum of seventy-five dollars ($75).
   Value received.

   George Brown (signature)

3. City, State, November 10, 19xx.
   Six months after date I promise to pay John Smith,
   Ralph White, or Jack Jackson, or order, one
   hundred dollars ($100).
   Value received.

   George Brown (signature)

4. City, State, November 10, 19xx.
   For value received, I promise to pay John Smith or
   order one hundred dollars ($100) when he shall be
   married.

   George Brown (signature)

5. If a bank fails before a certified check is paid, but after it is is certified, who loses? Why?

6. In order to be negotiable must a check be written in ink?

7. Would an otherwise correct check, made out to Mr. Miller, be rendered non-negotiable by striking out the words "or order" and substituting "or to anyone he designates"?

8. Would an otherwise correct check be negotiable if made out for only one cent?

9. Would an otherwise correct check be negotiable if made payable to the order of John Smith or his agent?

10. Would an otherwise correct promissory note made payable January 1, 2000, be negotiable?

11. In a bill of exchange, may the payee hold the drawer liable until the drawee accepts it?

PROFESSIONAL PUBLICATIONS, INC., P.O. Box 199, San Carlos, CA 94070

12.   Is a bank draft a bill of exchange?

13.   Must a bank draft be presented for acceptance before becoming negotiable?

14.   Does failure to present a check for payment within a reasonable time relieve the drawer from liability?

15.   John Smith gives Ed Brown a check to cancel a debt. Brown negotiates the check to Bob Jones, who in turn endorses it over to Smith to pay a debt owed by Jones to Smith. Will this last transaction discharge the instrument without the necessity of taking it to the bank for payment?

16.   Ralph Gordon delivers to Berman ten pictures to be framed. Berman's shop burns while the pictures are still in Berman's possession, and they are damaged. Upon whom does the loss fall? Why?

17.   Bill Carson owned some land that was mortgaged to Bob Jordan. Carson erected a building on this land in which he installed heavy machinery and boilers. At the time he intended these fixtures to be permanent. The machinery was fastened to the floor, and the boilers were set in masonry. Carson failed in the enterprise, and Jordan foreclosed. Carson sought to remove the machinery as personal property. Decide the case.

18.   Before warm weather set in, Gary Nelson had all his house screens sent to Tyler's shop for painting and repairing. Before the job was done, Nelson sold his house to Bob Gardner. To whom do the screens rightfully belong? Why?

19.   Bob lost a topcoat, practically new, from his car. Jack found it and sold it to Lynn for value. Later, Bob recognized the coat and was able to identify it. Could Bob force Lynn to surrender the coat? Why?

20.   William Barnett, a wholesale dealer in electrical supplies, receives from S. Kaiser a consignment of transformers with instructions to hold them until Kaiser's special agent arrives. Barnett, however, sells the transformers to Jay O'Leary before Kaiser's special agent arrives. Does O'Leary get a good title? Why?

21.   The City Electric Company sends a man to Bill Ketchum's pole yard to purchase 50 poles. This man examines a pile of 200 poles and agrees to purchase 50 of them and to call for them the next day. He leaves without designating the particular 50 he wishes to purchase. That night the yard catches fire and the poles are burned. Upon whom does the loss fall? Why? If the Electric Company's man had marked with marking crayon the 50 poles he desired, would this have made any difference? Why?

22.   Roger Gardner goes into Sam Brady's electrical-appliance store and examines an electric refrigerator. Brady tells him it is the best machine for the money on the market and that it runs as quietly as a watch and uses almost no energy. Gardner buys the refrigerator and

PROFESSIONAL PUBLICATIONS, INC., P.O. Box 199, San Carlos, CA 94070

discovers that the box is noisy and inefficient. Do Brady's statements constitute a warranty? Why?

23. Dick Lewis, a contractor, bought 50 tons of gravel from the Acme Gravel Company. At the time when the agreement was entered into, the Acme Gravel Company had furnished a sample run of gravel. After the 50 tons of gravel had been delivered, Lewis discovered that it was dirty, while the sample had been clean, and that it had nearly twice as much large aggregate as the sample. Can Smith sue for breach of warranty? Why?

24. Earnest Charles, a fruitgrower in Florida, sells to S. Giese, a fruit merchant in Indiana, 100 cases of grapefruit. Fifty cases are in transit to Giese, and 50 are in Charles' packing house ready to ship, when Charles learns that Giese is bankrupt. What action may Charles take?

25. Suppose that the 50 cases of fruit in Problem 24 had arrived and had been delivered to Giese, but had not yet been disposed of. Would Charles still have the same recourse? Why?

26. Norman sold Thomas on Monday 100 lb. of copper wire at 20 cents a pound, for which Thomas was to call on Thursday. Thomas refused to get the wire or pay for it. On Saturday, Norman sold the wire to Richard at the then market price of 15 cents per pound. Discuss Norman's recourses, if any.

27. Sam Wallace, a retail hardware merchant, purchased an assortment of nuts, bolts, and screws from Bob Barrett. When the shipment arrived, Wallace found one gross too few of type A screws, and one gross too many of type B nuts; in a sack with type C bolts, he found a number of type D bolts, not ordered, mixed in with the bolts ordered. What recourses does he have?

28. Jeff Mathews ordered from Joe Reiner 100 motors to be built to certain specifications. When the motors were ready, Mathews went to Reiner's plant, witnessed certain tests, and stated that the motors were satisfactory. He then left and the next day notified Reiner that he had changed his mind and did not want the motors. What action should Reiner take? Why?

29. The plaintiffs are co-partners in the building business. The defendant is a corporation having charge and control of public schools and school property in a large city. This defendant had a well-known rule in regard to buildings, by which it was provided that all new buildings should "be let by contract to the lowest and best bidder." The defendant advertised for bids for the erection of a new high school. The advertisement included the ordinary information with the last sentence reading "The Board reserves the right to reject any or all bids." The plaintiffs submitted a bid in strict compliance with the advertisement to build the proposed high school for $196,965. The defendant rejected the plaintiff's bid and accepted the bid of another for $197,000. The plaintiffs sued for alleged loss of profits in the sum of $15,000. Decide the case.

30. Joe Conrad tells his friend Fred Miller that he would sell his surveying transit to Rick Allen for $275 and Miller, without authority, tells Allen

about this. Can Allen hold Conrad to the offer?

31. If Steve Jason tells Tom Baxter that he might sell his (Jason's) factory this summer, is this an offer to which Baxter may hold Jason?

32. R. White told B. Jones he would sell him some cement. Nothing was said as to what cement was involved, where it was located, or what its price was. Is this an offer?

33. Collins vs. Jackson was an action to recover services for removing a stack of wheat kept on the plaintiff's (Collins) field by the defendant, Jackson. The defendant had promised to remove the wheat prior to plowing by Collins. The plaintiff, relying on Jackson's promise, set fire to the field to clear it for plowing and later discovered that the wheat had not been removed. To save the wheat, Collins removed it and sought to recover for the labor. Decide the case.

34. Jones wrote Green saying, "I will sell you 100 five-ampere alternating current meters at $18 each." After considering the offer for a day, Green wrote Jones accepting the offer and actually posted the letter. A half hour later Green received a telegram withdrawing the offer. Can Green hold Jones to the offer?

35. On April 20, a letter reached Sam Bowman from Tim Campbell containing an offer and indicating that the offer must be accepted on or before April 25. Assume that Bowman writes a properly phrased letter of acceptance on April 23. Is the acceptance binding in each of the following cases? (a) The letter reaches Campbell on April 24. (b) The letter reaches Campbell's office on April 24, but his secretary fails to give it to Campbell until April 26. (c) The letter is delayed in the mail and does not reach Campbell until April 27. (d) Campbell's secretary fails to post the letter until April 26. (e) A letter from Campbell withdrawing the offer reaches Bowman after he has posted his letter, but before it reaches Campbell.

36. Suppose that, in Problem 35, Bowman had telegraphed his acceptance. Would the acceptance be binding in each of the following cases? (a) The telegram reaches Campbell on April 24. (b) The telegram reaches Campbell on April 26. (c) The telegram reaches Campbell's city on April 24, but the local telegraph ofice fails to deliver the telegram until April 26. (d) The telegram reaches Campbell's office on April 24, but Campbell's office force fails to give it to Campbell until April 26.

37. R. Atkins wrote a letter dated May 29 offering 50 type S electric refrigerators with white enamel finish at $150 each, adding that acceptance must be made on or before June 10. K. Sellens replied by letter posted June 7, saying "I accept your offer of May 29 for 50 type S electric refrigerators provided that 25 of them are finished in cream-colored enamel." Is this acceptance binding? Why? (b) Atkins replied to Sellens that he could not furnish type S refrigerators in cream color. Sellens then telegraphed Atkins accepting all white refrigerators. This telegram reached Atkins on June 9. In the meantime Atkins had disposed of the refrigerators elsewhere. Had Atkins the right to dispose of the refrigerators before June 10? Why?

38. At 10 a.m., Charles Hoit received a telegram from Ray Stanton offering

PROFESSIONAL PUBLICATIONS, INC., P.O. Box 199, San Carlos, CA 94070

a special price on ten air-conditioning units. Later, Hoit left his office and, after attending to certain business matters, dropped into the telegraph office and sent a telegram to Stanton accepting his offer. This telegram was stamped "Received at 12:15 p.m." Upon returning to his office at 1:30 p.m., Hoit found a telegram stamped "Delivered at 11:30 a.m." from Stanton withdrawing the offer. Was Hoit's acceptance binding? Why?

39. The AC Power Company asked for bids on a new plant. A number of bidders sent in bids. When the bids were opened, Keefer's bid was the lowest. The president of the power company met Keefer on the street and said, "You are the lucky man." Keefer understood by this statement that a written agreement would be entered into later and made preparations to begin the construction. Later, the power company officials became doubtful of Keefer's ability and gave the contract to another. Could Keefer recover for breach of contract? If so, why?

40. Tim Martin leased a warehouse from Larry Rossen. Rossen told Martin that the building would be ready for him on March 1. On March 2, Martin took possession of the building and started to move in a quantity of goods when he discovered several cases of merchandise belonging to Rossen. He removed these cases and then sought to collect from Rossen for the expense of removing them. Could he collect? Why?

41. (a) Steve Jacobs, while driving, passed Clint Warner, who was having engine trouble. Jacobs stopped and assisted Warner in getting his car started, but in the process ruined a suit of clothes. Later Jacobs sued Warner for the price of the suit. Could he collect? Why? (b) Suppose that Jacobs had been hurt and sought to recover medical expenses. Could he collect in this case? Why?

42. On June 1, the Board of Directors of the AC Power Company met. The following statement appeared in the minutes of this meeting: "Mr. Bogart moved that the Gessit Appraisal Company be given the contract to make the valuation of our B Street plant. Seconded by Mr. Kirk and passed." Nothing further was done about it, and the Gessit Company brought suit for breach of contract, basing its claim on the minutes stated above. Could the Gessit Company collect? Why?

43. Farmer Brown captures and turns over to the authorities a suspicious character whom he has found hiding in his barn. This man turns out to be a criminal for whom a reward for capture has been posted. Could Farmer Brown collect the reward? Why?

44. M. Benson inherited a piece of land, worth about $8,000 from an uncle. Benson's father induced him to deed the land to Benson, senior, for $2,000. Young Benson was of age and brought the case to a court of equity. What would be the court's decision? If young Benson had instead been simple-minded or old and weak-minded and had been induced to sell to a real-estate agent, what then? Finally, suppose Benson to be the only son of a wealthy man and in dire need of funds. H. Sherman, a moneylender agrees to loan Benson, who is 21 years of age, $1,000 if he (Benson) will legally make an assignment of his rights to his father's estate. Believing himself helpless, Benson

signs such a document. Later, the case is placed in a court of equity. What will be the court's decision?

45. Pascalli had a beautiful Oriental rug with a blue background. Being in need of ready cash, he went to Madsen, a furniture dealer, and offered him the rug for $500. Madsen replied in the presence of witnesses that he remembered the rug well, for he had recently delivered furniture at Pascalli's home, that he knew of a customer who was in the market for such a rug, and that he would therefore be glad to give Pascalli $500 for it. It developed later that Madsen had thought all the time that the rug had a brown background and, since his customer did not want one with a blue background, he refused to buy. Pascalli sued. Madsen set up the defense of mistake. Is the defense good? Why?

46. Gene Frank contracted to buy a residence from Bill Compson. He planned to make a two-family house out of it and rent one side while living in the other. Before signing the agreement to purchase, both Frank and Compson examined the property and agreed that the plan was feasible. Before final payments were made, Frank discovered that a zoning law would prevent him from making the house over as he had planned and he declined to buy. Compson sued. Frank set up the defense of mutual mistake. Was the defense good? Why?

47. Corey purchased certain stocks from Simon upon the latter's representation of the present and future value of the stock. The evidence showed that the statements were false and made with the intent of causing Corey to buy; but the evidence also showed that Corey had disposed of the stocks for enough more than he had paid for them to cover the interest on his money for the period in which they were in his possession. In a suit charging fraud, would Corey be successful? Why?

48. Bert Collins forged the name of his father to a note. Upon discovery of the forgery, the bank informed the father that, if the latter did not countersign the note, the bank would expose the son as a felon and turn the matter over to the authorities. Is a note signed under such conditions binding? Why?

49. E. Ritter, an aged widow with several living children, with whom she was on the best of terms, met a young man in his early twenties. She had known this man for only about six months when she deeded all her real property to him, thus disinheriting her own children. What redress at law would the children have, if any?

50. John told Rick that his car was a 1947 model, although he was aware that it was a 1946 model; he made the statement falsely, knowing that Rick was a good friend of Sam, who was in the market for a 1947 model like that owned by John. Sam bought the car from John on the strength of Rick's statement. John made no statement to Sam about the model of the car. When Sam discovered that the car was a 1946 model, he sued John, charging fraud. Could he recover? Why?

51. Don Moore tells Peter Smith, in order to induce him to buy, that a certain lot is the best buy in the city, that the city is sure to expand in the direction of the lot and that, if he keeps it three or four years,

PROFESSIONAL PUBLICATIONS, INC., P.O. Box 199, San Carlos, CA 94070

it will at least double its present value. Smith buys; the city expands in another direction; and two years later the lot is worth only half what it was worth when purchased. Smith sues Moore, charging fraud. Can he recover? Why?

52. Dan Hoffman had a valuable dog, which he said before witnesses was 3 years old. Charles Turner, who was present, purchased the dog. After the purchase, it was discovered that the dog was 5 years old. Which of the following conditions would support an action for damages, and why? (a) Hoffman honestly believed the dog was 3 years old. (b) Turner knew Hoffman was wrong at the time of the purchase. (c) Hoffman made the statement falsely, but Turner could not prove that he had suffered any loss by the transaction. (d) Hoffman's statement was a general one made to the group without any intention of defrauding any particular individual. (e) Turner was unable to show that the statement in any way influenced his decision to buy.

53. Dick Lewis, a contractor, offered to install additional outlets in Bert Simpson's house for the cost of materials during his spare time. Simpson accepted, and the work was completed. Some time after the work was done, Lewis had occasion to need Simpson's services; Simpson at first agreed to furnish said services in consideration for what Lewis had done, but later refused, claiming lack of consideration. Decide the case.

54. Suppose that Mark Denton is a personal friend of the district attorney and that Natt Kerr's son has just been arrested for speeding. Kerr agrees to give Denton the contract for wiring Kerr's new house if Denton will get his friend, the district attorney, to reduce his son's fine. Denton is successful in getting the fine reduced, but Kerr refuses to keep his promise, claiming lack of consideration. Discuss the case.

55. Bill McFadden offered to sell Ellen Martin an antique desk he had for $20. Martin accepted, paid the $20, and went to get a truck to remove the desk. In the meantime, Tom Boswell told McFadden that the desk was worth as least $100; when Martin returned, McFadden took back the $20, and refused to deliver the desk, claiming insufficient consideration. Decide the case.

56. Shawn O'Hennessy met and became well acquainted with a young man, Tim O'Casey. As Mr. O'Hennessy had no descendants, he wished to perpetuate the name of O'Hennessy and proposed to Mr. O'Casey that the latter legally change his name O'Hennessy; in consideration for this act, the first Mr. O'Hennessy would turn over to the new Mr. O'Hennessy a considerable fortune. Mr. O'Hennessy the second agreed to this arrangement and took the necessary legal steps. At this point, Mr. O'Hennessy the first became doubtful of the merits of his bargain and refused to turn over the fortune promised, claiming lack of consideration. Was the defense good? Why?

57. Bob owed Joe $8,000 for goods delivered and accepted. This amount appeared on the books of both persons. Despairing of receiving the whole $8,000, Bob accepted a note for $4,000 secured by a chattel mortgage on the personal property of Joe in full payment for the $8,000. The note was paid on time, and the chattel mortgage was satisfied. However, Bob brought suit for the balance of the original

PROFESSIONAL PUBLICATIONS, INC., P.O. Box 199, San Carlos, CA 94070

debt of $8,000. Could he recover? Why?

58. Sid Galt claimed that when Jean Kerock died, the later owed the former $1,000. Kerock's relatives claimed that the debt was for $500. Neither side was able to prove that the amount it named was correct. Fisher, the administrator for Kerock, promised in writing to settle the matter by paying Galt $750 out of the estate. Galt agreed to this compromise. Later, however, he changed his mind and sued for the additional $250, claiming that his agreement was without consideration. Decide the case.

59. Eddie Milton is in possession of damaging information against Murray Jacobs, who is being tried for a crime. Jess Harper, a friend of Jacobs offers to pay Milton $1,000 if Milton will refrain from testifying at Jacobs' trial. Eddie at first agrees, then changes his mind and testifies. Harper sues Jacobs. Can he recover? Why?

60. John Seidel, a recent graduate in electrical engineering, built up a going business in radios and radio repairs in his home town of 5,000 inhabitants. He sold his business and good will to Hugh Dow for $5,000 and agreed not to enter into that or a similar business within the state. Later he moved to the capital of the state 60 miles away from his home town and started the same kind of business. When Dow heard about this, he brought suit claiming breach of contract. Decide the case.

61. The Acme Company was low bidder on a sewer to be constructed for Gotham City. Acme was awarded the contract and completed the sewer. The amount involved was $50,000. The city accepted the work. At this point, Jones, a taxpaying citizen of the city, brought suit to enjoin the city from paying any part of the $50,000 on the ground that Acme Company had violated an old statute that prohibited any company employed on state or municipal work from working labor more than 8 hours a day. The evidence showed that the Acme Company had employed some of their men for occasional work lasting longer than 8 hours a day. Decide the case.

62. Kent Holmes contracted orally with Don Glass, sales manager of the Kool Refrigerator Company to sell refrigerators at $150 each until the supply of 500 was exhausted. The salary was to be $300 a month and expenses. Three months after Holmes started work, and before all the refrigerators were sold, Glass discharged Holmes. Holmes sued, and Glass set up the defense that the contract came under the fourth section of the Statute of Frauds as requiring more than a year to complete. The trial judge ruled in favor of Glass. Holmes then appealed, and the appellate judge changed the decision of the trial judge on the grounds that the case came under the seventeenth section of the Statute of Frauds as being for the sale of goods in excess of $50. The case then went to the supreme court of the state, where the decision was uniformly for Holmes. Discuss the three decisions as to their correctness.

63. In an oral agreement, Billingsley obtained permission from Haskinso to dig and carry away ore at $5 a ton from a mine belonging to Haskins. Billinsley bought some machinery and prepared to operate the mine. Then Haskins refused to let Billingsley proceed. Can Billingsley force

Haskins to live up to his agreement? Why?

64. Eric Bass had an oil well from which Bob Brown himself pumped and barreled 10 bbl. of oil a day. Bass agreed with Brown to sell Brown a year's output at $1 a barrel. After 6 months, Bass sold the well outright to Cliff Castle; when Brown sued, he set up the defense that his agreement with Bass was for an interest in real estate and therefore came under the Statute of Frauds. Decide the case.

65. Andy Carmichael agreed orally with Joe McCoy to haul dirt in McCoy's yard and to plant lawn for $45. Carmichael later refused to complete the job, and when McCoy sued, set up as a defense the Statute of Frauds. Is this a good defense? Why?

66. Will Johnson contracted with the Acme Construction Company to act as its engineer for 1 year from the coming June. After 6 months, he was discharged. If Johnson is to be successful in a suit for breach of contract, what must he produce, and why?

67. P. Clark, a salesman, received an oral order for 100 desk lamps from B. Lee In each case, state with reasons whether Lee can be held for the order: (a) Clark leaves with Lee two demonstration lamps, which Lee accepts as part of the order. (b) Clark gives Lee a kitchen-lamp unit in appreciation of the order. (c) Clark can produce correspondence in which the number ordered and the price to be paid are mentioned. (d) Lee gives Clark $25 in advance payment on the order.

68. The Lift Elevator Company contracted to install an elevator in Clifton's store under the agreement that if it was not completely satisfactory to Clifton, the Lift Elevator Company would remove it at its own expense. Clifton was not satisfied. In a suit, a nationally known elevator engineer testified that the installation in every respect was strictly in accordance with the best engineering practice for the class of service involved. Would Brown have to pay? Why?

69. G. Broderick, a contractor, completed a building for P. Clinton, a private citizen. The specifications called for 6-inch drains in the basement. Owing to the contractor's error, 4-inch drains were installed. Discuss the relative rights of both parties, the type of case involved, what court it would be tried in, and the principle under which it would be decided.

70. The Acme Company engaged the services of J. Roades, a young mechanical engineer, to make an efficiency survey of its factory and to rearrange it according to the best modern practice. He was to start June 1. On June 1, Roades reported to start the job, but the Acme Company had just received a rush order and told Roades he would have to wait. Roades then started another job with the Boeing Company and, when the Acme Company notified Roades that it was ready, Roades told the officers of the Acme Company that they would have to wait another month until he had finished the Boeing Company job. Can Roades be held for breach of contract? Why?

71. Bob Lindley, an engineer with a considerable reputation as a successful designer of small reinforced-concrete filling stations, contracted with the Eazy Oil Company for twenty-five such stations. He then lost

interest in the proposition and assigned all his rights to Glascoe, another equally successful engineer. Eazy Oil Company then brought suit to compel specific performance on the contract. Decide the case.

72. B&O Railroad Company entered into an agreement with Gotham City to use a certain city street while eliminating a grade crossing. The agreement stipulated that the street was to be restored to its original condition after the work had been completed. The railroad company found it necessary to make a retaining wall that decreased the width of the street. In a suit by the city, the railroad claimed impossibility of performance. Decide the case.

73. Is a principal required to reimburse an agent for a fine incurred by the agent as a result of the agent running through a red traffic light while on the business of the agency?

74. Is a principal required to reimburse an agent for damages resulting from a successful suit brought by a person for damages to that person's car caused by one of the agency's trucks skidding on a slippery pavement while being driven by an authorized driver of the agency who was not negligent?

75. Must a principal fulfill an agreement made by his general agent with a third party, even though the agent has had written instructions not to make such an agreement, but said instructions were not known to the third party?

76. Is a principal obligated in the following situation: Smith told Brown that Green was his agent, and empowered to sell his truck. Brown had a passenger car in excellent condition, which he persuaded Green to accept in trade for the truck that Smith had given Green to sell.

77. On May 23, Stuart Taylor informed Jack Aker, the agent of Frank Earle, that certain perishable goods were ready to deliver, but Aker forgot to tell Earle about this until May 28. When Earle collected the goods on May 31, he refused to accept some of the said goods because they were spoiled. Can Taylor hold Earle for the spoiled goods if he so desires?

78. Peter Lindsay represents himself to William Winter as an electrical engineering graduate with 5 years' experience in industrial applications and is hired as Winter's agent. Lindsay recommends that Joe Blemm purchase six squirrel-cage four-pole 60-cycle induction motors to operate paper mills that must run at 1,800 r.p.m. Can Winter hold Lindsay personally responsible if the motors fail to operate the mills at the required speed?

79. Paul Cox employed Joe Cornell as his agent to sell a certain house for Smith for which Cox was to receive $300. After Cox and Cornell had signed their agreement, but before Cornell had done any work, the house was destroyed by fire. Could Cornell hold Cox for the $300?

80. L. Wallace, of Center City, while in Pinedale heard Jerry Smythe testify under oath in a court trial in Pinedale that Tom Cutter was his agent in Center City and was empowered to represent him in all business affairs in Center City. Wallace contracted with Cutter for the

roofing of a certain building, using Smythe's shingles. The shingles proved defective, and Wallace sued Smythe. In the testimony it was proved that Cutter was not Smythe's agent and never had been. Cutter made no mention, expressed or implied, that he was agent for Smythe, and Wallace had made no other inquiries elsewhere. In deciding the case, was the judge correct in ruling that Smythe v/as liable?

81. Lou Brown, professing to act as an agent for John Smith, entered into an agreement with Bob White. As a matter of fact, Brown had no authority to act for Smith. Hearing about the agreement, Smith came forward and created Brown his agent in the matter by ratification. White then refused to fulfill his part of the agreement and Smith sued. Under the law of agency, should Smith be successful in his suit?

82. Will McKay is an engineer and an agent of the Acme Company. The agreement creating the agency is legally correct in all particulars. He is instructed to pay up to, but not in excess of, $500,000 for all the land necessary on a certain watershed to enable the company to build a dam and hydroelectric plant of a certain capacity. In each of the following cases, discuss the legality of the act and the liabilities and rights of all parties involved, i.e., principal, agent, subagent, and third parties: (a) The engineer purchases land that is not at all necessary. (b) By careful buying, he accomplishes the job at a total cost of $450,000 and keeps the balance of the $500,000 allowed. (c) After making the survey, designating the land, and fixing the maximum to be paid for each tract, McKay employs Fred Richards, who is a better bargainer, to do the actual buying. (d) Without making the survey and the other steps taken in situation (c), McKay employs Kurt Miller, a competent engineer, to do it for him. Miller's total is well under $500,000. (e) McKay is not able to buy the rights needed for $500,000, but does get them for $600,000. The Acme Company starts building the dam and power plant and then refuses to make good to McKay for the additional $100,000. (f) Assume the same conditions as in (e), except that the Acme Company refuses from the outset to ratify McKay's total of $600,000. (g) McKay employs Carson to act as chainman on the survey. Carson makes a bad mistake. (h) A truck operated by McKay kills a cow owned by Johnson. At the time the truck was being used on business of the agency and was driven by Carson, but Carson was not negligent. (i) Carson enters Johnson's house and steals the latter's watch. (j) McKay is injured while engaged in the business of the agency.

83. Jones, a contractor, was hired by W. Mapes on a time and material basis to build a home on Mapes' property. Jones hired a professional engineer to supervise the construction. Jones leased equipment, and his foreman instructed and controlled the operator of the equipment. The operator negligently permitted the equipment to overheat, thus causing an explosion and injury to a passerby. The passerby sues the owner, contractor, foreman, operator, engineer, and equipment-renting company. Who, if anybody, is liable?

84. Steve Baxter contracted with Mr. Balin to build a $20,000 warehouse. The next day, Baxter had a serious heart attack that incapacitated him from working. Is Baxter excused? Explain.

85. Andy Seacole sells Barry Lawson a secondhand engine, delivery of

PROFESSIONAL PUBLICATIONS, INC., P.O. Box 199, San Carlos, CA 94070

which Lawson accepts and pays for. Seacole, in offering the engine for sale, represented it would deliver 50 brake H.P. Lawson now states the engine will not develop 50 brake H.P. and had he known this he would not have bought it. Can Lawson compel Seacole to take back the engine and refund his money?

PROFESSIONAL PUBLICATIONS, INC., P.O. Box 199, San Carlos, CA 94070

PART II: PRODUCT SAFETY AND DESIGN LIABILITY

When discussing the liability of engineers, one must distinguish between *design professionals* (e.g., building designers and architects) and *product designers.* Degign professionals are generally consultants. They may or may not work for a large consulting firm. Their primary product is a design service, and this service is sold to a specific client. Product designers generally work for a company that manufactures a specific product line, which is sold through retailers to multiple consumers.

The law treats design professionals in a favorable manner. Such professionals are expected to meet a standard of care and skill that can be measured by comparison to the conduct of other professionals; they are not expected to be infallible. In the absence of a contract provision to the contrary, design professionals are not held to be guarantors of their work in the strict sense of legal liability.

On the other hand, the law is much stricter with product manufacturers and perfection is expected of them. They are held to the standard of *strict liability in tort.* This is without regard to negligence. A manufacturer is held liable for all phases of design and manufacturing of a product being marketed to the public.

The discussion in this chapter of product safety and design liability combines design professionals and product designers in a general discussion of liability. In general, courts are much stricter on product designers and manufacturers than on design professionals.

1. LEGAL RESPONSIBILITIES OF ENGINEERS

The liability of engineers depends on a number of factors. There is generally an implied liability for competent design and testing. In addition, engineers may have implied or contractual reponsibilities of supervision and/or inspection.

- Supervision. Where specific contractual clauses require design professionals to "supervise," courts have held that those design professionals were liable for defects that could have been detected by adequate supervision.

- Inspection. "Inspection" has been interpreted by the courts, in some cases, to mean exhaustive and continuous inspection of all project details. Design professionals typically do only observation and spot checking.

- Testing. Courts have repeatedly held that new materials must be thoroughly tested before being incorporated into a design. Tests may be done by design professionals or by independent labs, as long as the test results are considered reliable by most other professionals. Sole reliance on sales literature and manufacturers' claims is inadequate.

PROFESSIONAL PUBLICATIONS, INC., P.O. Box 199, San Carlos, CA 94070

- Design. Most liability cases center on defective, inadequate design.

- Whistle Blowing. Engineers must constantly struggle with management to prevent the development of unsafe practices or defective conditions. Mere awareness or notification of management about the condition is insufficient.

  If management fails to take action about potentially dangerous conditions, an engineer has a moral and legal responsibility to take further action. Only this action can minimize his own personal liability.

2. HISTORY OF DESIGN LIABILITY TRENDS

Liability laws are not static, and the growing awareness in this country of the need to provide stricter controls on consumer products has resulted in stricter liability judgments. The following cases show how attitudes and laws have changed.

- 1842, England, Winterbottom vs. Wright. Wright had a contract with the owner of a vehicle that required Wright to maintain the vehicle. Winterbottom was a passenger of Wright's who was injured by the vehicle's state of disrepair. Winterbottom's suit against Wright cited poor maintenance, but was denied by the judge since Wright's maintenance contract was with the vehicle owner, not with Winterbottom. This is known as *prerequisite of privity,* meaning that there must be a face-to-face contractual relationship between two parties before there can be liability.

- 1916, McPherson vs. Buick. McPherson bought a Buick from a dealer. The car had a defective steering wheel, and there was evidence that reasonable inspection would have uncovered the defect. The wooden steering wheel injured McPherson, who sued Buick. Buick defended itself under the prerequisite of privity since the dealer had sold the car to McPherson and no contract between Buick and McPherson existed. The judge disagreed, thus establishing the concept that manufacturers are responsible to consumers. This is known as *third party liability.*

- 1958, Maroevich vs. Irving. Irving was a notary public who failed to have Maroevich's will attested to by two witnesses when signed by Maroevich. Since this was contrary to state law, the court later failed to recognize the will. Maroevich's sister received one-eighth of what the will had left her, and she sued Irving, even though she was not Irving's client. The court found Irving liable, despite the lack of privity. Thus, third party liability was extended to service contracts (such as those used by design professionals).

- 1960, Henningsen vs. Bloomfield Motors. This decision ruled that disclaimers regarding safety are invalid and that an implied warranty was in effect between the product user and the manufacturer.

PROFESSIONAL PUBLICATIONS, INC., P.O. Box 199, San Carlos, CA 94070

- 1963, Greenman vs. Yuba Power Products. This case was based on a personal injury resulting from the use of a combination electric power tool. The court ruled that "a manufacturer is strictly liable in tort when an article he places on the market, knowing that it will be used without inspection, proves to have a defect that causes injury to a human being." This decision established the doctrine of *strict liability in tort.*

In summary, prior to 1916 the legal and judicial posture towards product defects was exemplified by the expression *Caveat Emptor,* or "Let the Buyer Beware." Subsequent court rulings have brought about a specific change towards greater consumer protection.

This does not imply that absolute liability is being imposed on manufacturers. The plaintiff still must prove certain facts to the satisfaction of the courts (e.g., the product was defective, unreasonably dangerous, etc.). These are specific conditions that manufacturers can guard against by designing, manufacturing, and marketing a safe product.

3. CATEGORIES OF DEFECTIVE PRODUCTS

A. Manufacturing Defect

This is a defect in a product resulting from a miscarriage of the manufacturing process. Other products made by the same process may not be defective, in which case the defective item is the result of poor quality control and insufficient inspection. If all products of a certain type are defective, it is usually a result of either a flaw in the manufacturing process or a defect in the design of the product.

B. Design Defect

A product is said to have a design defect if the intended design of the product can be shown or found to make the product not reasonably safe. Over the years, legal findings have gradually evolved a definition of a defective design. A defective design is characterized by one or more of the following features:

- The manufacturer has failed to do everything necessary to make the product function properly for the purpose for which it was designed.

- The product has a latent defect.

- The functioning of the product creates danger that is unknown to the user.

Examples of defective products are:

- Toy ovens with exposed hot surfaces that burn children.

- A toy bazooka that deafens a child playmate of the user.

- Wringer washing machines that catch the hands and arms of

unwary users.

- Power tools that cause injury because of lack of effective guards against whirling gears, chains, teeth, blades, or flying fragments.

- Baby furniture that causes infant strangulation.

- Floor furnaces with exposed hot surfaces on which children are burned.

- Rotary lawnmowers that throw rocks and other objects hidden in the grass.

4. TYPES OF PRODUCT LIABILITY SUITS

A. Strict Liability in Tort

Liability cases are tort cases because they involve personal injury. The plaintiff wins if he proves injury by a defective and unreasonably dangerous product. This requires the plaintiff to prove all of the following:

- Product was defective when used.

- Product was defective when manufactured.

- Product was unreasonably dangerous.

- Defect caused his injury.

- The specific use of the product that caused the damage was reasonably foreseeable.

It is not necessary to prove breach of warranty or privity of contract. Nor is it necessary to prove designer negligence. The defect itself, regardless of how it got there, is sufficient to create liability in tort.

Design professionals are seldom individually named in strict liability suits. Usually the manufacturing company is charged.

B. Design-Related Liability

A defective design is caused by an individual's oversight or poor judgment during the design process. Criminal charges may be brought if the designer willingly or knowingly acted fraudulently or in a way that might bring personal harm to product users. Otherwise, civil proceedings, usually in the form of a simple negligence case, are appropriate if the design flaw was unintentional and undetected until injury had been sustained by the product user.

Examples of cases where criminal charges can be brought against an engineer for fraudulent actions or misconduct are:

- He knowingly selected and applied unsafe design practices.

- He knowingly incorporated unsafe devices in the design.

- He participated in a cover-up of product failure or unsatisfactory testing results.

Courts have ruled that engineers have a moral responsibility to users of their products. Being ordered by a supervisor to act fraudulently, even when such orders are in writing, is not a satisfactory defense. In such cases, the engineer should "blow the whistle."

Negligence charges are more easily proven than criminal actions. Examples of negligence are:

- Failure to remove safety-device override mechanisms used during assembly or testing.

- Incorrect labeling.

- Faulty calculation in design or test.

- Failure to read a report from a subordinate showing a defect.

- Failure to install adequate safety devices, such as guards, fail-safe switches, interlocks, monitoring equipment, and safety valves.

- Use of safety devices that do not work.

- Lack of adequate testing after product is manufactured.

- Use of inadequate materials.

- A manufacturing process that leads to a defective product.

- Failure to plan for foreseeable uses not intended by the manufacturer or to anticipate the consequences of ordinary wear and tear or improper maintenance.

- Addition of unnecessary parts.

- Failure to keep abreast of scientific knowledge, advanced testing procedures, or industry standards.

Negligence evidence is frequently accumulated during *discovery proceedings.* Under current discovery procedures, lawyers for the plaintiff may ask questions about design, request any existing documents, tour the factory, and search files. This makes it easy to implicate design professionals who may be named in addition to their companies as co-defendants in these cases.

C. Industry-Wide Liability

An entire industry may be liable if the original manufacturer cannot be determined, or if the entire industry designs to the same standards. An example of this is a wrongful death suit filed by the widow of an asbestos worker against all asbestos manufacturers.

PROFESSIONAL PUBLICATIONS, INC., P.O. Box 199, San Carlos, CA 94070

D. Comparative Liability

Defendants may be able to claim some defense in cases where the plaintiff is partly to blame for injuries sustained from the product. Although the laws in *comparative negligence* cases differ from state to state, most courts allow the defendant to collect a part of his claim if he is partly, but strictly less than half, to blame for the injury. If the plaintiff knew about and ignored the defect, or if he is more than 50% to blame for the injury, no award is made.

The extremes of comparative negligence laws range from *contributory negligence* (where plaintiffs cannot recover any damages at all if they were responsible to any degree) to *pure comparative negligence* (where plaintiffs can recover damages to the extent they were not responsible). Pure comparative negligence, as present in California law, does not have the 50% limitation.

5. STRATEGIES FOR PROTECTION AGAINST LIABILITY SUITS

The best protection against liability suits is competent work and professional design practices. However, even the most careful designers make mistakes, and it is the nature of the profession that the engineer is in a somewhat vulnerable position as far as liability goes. The following steps may help to ensure that the engineer is protected as much as possible from lawsuits and the resultant financial burden of a lost lawsuit.

- Errors and omissions insurance. Often a major expense for design professionals, insurance will not cover fraudulent or willful design defects, only "honest" errors.

- Incorporation of the business. Service-oriented design professionals who do all their work through a self-founded corporation may risk their corporate assets, but their personal assets are generally safe.

- Working for a product-oriented corporation. Engineers who work for corporations that produce products are exempt from most licensing laws and are seldom listed as co-defendants in product liability suits. The manufacturing company is the primary defendant.

- Going Bare. Design professionals may choose not to carry errors and omissions insurance. Such professionals typically assign all of their assets to a corporation or spouse to keep them from being entangled in liability losses. Product liability suits are seldom filed against individuals or companies that have little or nothing in the way of ability to pay off awards. Courts are reluctant to reduce any individual to pauper status for the purpose of paying off liability awards.

- Contract Clauses. In some cases, design professionals can eliminate their liability by having their clients consent to a *hold harmless agreement,* which releases the engineer from liability.

PROFESSIONAL PUBLICATIONS, INC., P.O. Box 199, San Carlos, CA 94070

6. CAUSES OF LIABILITY SUITS

The causes of negligence suits are seemingly endless. The following list gives some examples of reasons why suits have been brought against manufacturers and design professionals.

- True design errors (accidental errors).

- Failure to install or specify safety devices.

- Use of defective or inadequately designed safety devices.

- Construction from unsafe materials.

- Defects from the manufacturing process.

- Failure to plan for foreseeable uses not intended by the manufacturer.

- Failure to foresee consequences of ordinary use or improper maintenance.

- Use of unnecessary parts.

- Failure to measure up to industry standards.

- Failure to keep abreast of scientific knowledge.

- Failure to disclose all potential hazards to buyer.

7. SAFETY, RELIABILITY, AND QUALITY

Safety, reliability, and quality are not synonymous terms. A product or design may be highly reliable, but it may have a dangerous characteristic.

Safety is an implied warranty that the product, by being offered for sale or use, is reasonably safe to use. The implied warranty of safety is always in effect. No express warranty is needed. Further, the implied warranty of safety is not generally limited by the period in which the product is in use or by the type of damages or injury sustained if an accident occurs.

Reliability is usually an express warranty that the product will operate satisfactorily for a specific period of time. (For example, car manufacturers usually warranty their products for 20,000 miles or two years. This is an express reliability warranty.)   However, increasing reliability does not necessarily improve safety.

Quality is a term with statistical significance. 100% testing, also known as *exhaustive testing,* is seldom used in mass production products. Quality testing based on samples recognizes that a small fraction of defective products will exist. The quality of a product, then, can be measured by

PROFESSIONAL PUBLICATIONS, INC., P.O. Box 199, San Carlos, CA 94070

this fraction. Attributes of a product that can cause injury, however, should never be tested by sample unless the manufacturer is willing to take the statistical risk.

Consumer Warning Notices. Some products are inherently dangerous, despite all manufacturing and design care. For example, chain saws can still injure if improperly used, and bottles of poison may be misused by children.

In such instances, warning notices should be used to inform users of potential dangers. Such warning should be present in all instruction literature, but decals and labels should also carry the warnings on the product. In the case of products that will be used by non-English speaking individuals, such warnings should be written in multiple languages.

8. CONSUMER PRODUCT SAFETY ACT

The Consumer Product Safety Act (CPSA) of 1972 established a commission (The Consumer Product Safety Commission, CPSC) to administer the act and earlier laws regarding product safety. The CPSC also promulgates new consumer product safety standards through the Federal Register.

Section 15(b) of the CPSA states that every manufacturer of a consumer product distributed in commerce, and every distributor and retailer of such products who obtains information that reasonably supports the conclusion that a product contains a dangerous defect, shall immediately inform the Commission of that defect.

The Commission must be notified within 24 hours of discovery of the defect, and a written confirmation must be sent within 48 hours. Additional information regarding product identification, the nature of the defect, quantity in use, corrective action to be taken, and advice to sellers and purchasers is also required.

Section 15(b) deals with defects that could create (meaning potential) substantial public danger. Therefore, manufacturers may have difficulty in deciding whether a defect is serious enough to warrant reporting. Since such reports to the CPSC are public record and are often reported by the press, such a report would place a manufacturer in a poor competitive position.

Section 15(c) deals with public notification of the defect. Section 15(d) of the CPSA deals with product repair and replacement when a product presents substantial product hazard.

PROFESSIONAL PUBLICATIONS, INC., P.O. Box 199, San Carlos, CA 94070

REVIEW PROBLEMS FOR PART II

1. An engineer designs a building that is constructed according to plans and specifications. The building owner hires a window washer to wash the windows. When the window washer falls from the building, he sues the design engineer. Discuss this suit under the Winterbottom vs. Wright precedent. How would modern day courts decide such a case?

2. Discuss the 1975 case of Kent vs. Bartlett. Bartlett was a surveyor hired by Wisehart to survey property. Bartlett was instructed to subdivide property in such a manner as to isolate a building, wall, and driveway on one parcel, leaving the other parcel free of all rights of way. Bartlett completed the survey and filed his map. Wisehart sold the empty parcel to the Kents, and the Kents further sold the parcel to other purchasers. The new purchasers discovered the parcel map was in error, and part of the driveway and retaining wall prohibited using the parcel as intended. Kent paid off the purchasers and then sued Bartlett for the negligent survey. Prepare a defense for Bartlett. Kent won the case. Why?

3. An oceanside hotel hired an engineer to design a pier for sunbathers. The pier was constructed and no design flaws were encountered. However, bad weather, high waves, and surges prevented the hotel from opening the pier safely, despite the fact than an oceanographer had been part of the design team and had provided wave information. The hotel sued the engineer, but lost. Why?

4. A small child threw an aerosol can of hairspray into the family fireplace. The can exploded and injured the child. The child's father sued the hairspray manufacturer. The manufacturer defended itself by pointing out that the can had a warning not to incinerate. The father argued that the manufacturer should have anticipated that some cans would end up incinerated and that the can should have had a safe means of failure other than explosion. Who was right?

5. An aircraft designer specified titanium fasteners of the highest quality and strength when designing a connection. The manufacturer of the fastener used an inadequate quality sampling plan, and several defective fasteners caused structural failure of the connection. Discuss the liability of the designer, his company, and the fastener manufacturer.

6. A 1961 American compact car was designed so that a front-end cross member could get caught crossing railroad tracks not at a track intersection. If the driver of such a car is killed when he tries to cross a set of raised tracks, should the manufacturer be held liable?

7. A chemical insecticide was packaged in a bottle with many warning notices written in English. The bottle was misused by a migrant farm worker, who later died. The farm worker could not read English, nor was there a skull and crossbones on the bottle. The farm worker's widow won her case against the insecticide manufacturer. Discuss why she won.

PROFESSIONAL PUBLICATIONS, INC., P.O. Box 199, San Carlos, CA 94070

8. A university student was electrocuted in 1973 while taking a whirlpool bath in a field house that had been designed in 1955 and completed in 1958. The state had a 10-year statute of limitations to prevent stale claims against engineers and architects. The court and the state's supreme court dismissed the case against the building designer on the basis of the statute of limitations. Do you think that was appropriate?

PART III: PROFESSIONAL ETHICS

1. INTRODUCTION

Many different sets of codes and canons of ethics have been produced by various engineering societies and state registration boards. The purpose of these ethical codes is to guide the conduct of consulting engineers, and therefore, such codes are primarily educational. Nevertheless, they have been used by societies and registration boards as the basis for disciplinary action.

Fundamental to such ethical codes is the requirement for consulting engineers to render faithful professional service and to honestly represent the interests of their clients while, at the same time, protecting public health, safety, and welfare.

2. DEALING WITH CLIENTS

Although a typical set of ethical codes is included as an appendix, most of the client codes can be summarized in the following items.

- The consulting engineer should protect his client's interest. This protection goes beyond normal business relationships and transcends the legal requirements of the engineer-client contract.

- Confidential client information is kept confidential and remains the property of the client.

- The consulting engineer should avoid conflicts of interest and should inform his client of any business connections or interests that might influence the engineer's judgment.

- The consulting engineer should recognize his own limitations. He should use associates and other experts when the design requirements exceed his abilities.

- The consulting engineer should not accept discounts, allowances, commissions, or any other indirect compensation in connection with any work or recommendations. The engineer's sole source of income is the fee paid by his client.

- If the consulting engineer's recommendations are questioned or are not accepted, he will present the consequences clearly to the client.

- The consulting engineer will not be bound by what the client wants in instances where such a plan would be unsuccessful.

- The consulting engineer admits freely and openly any errors to his client.

PROFESSIONAL PUBLICATIONS, INC., P.O. Box 199, San Carlos, CA 94070

3. DEALING WITH CONTRACTORS AND SUPPLIERS

Consulting engineers, in carrying out their designs, must deal with contractors, manufacturers, and suppliers. In this regard, consulting engineers have great responsibility and power. Such a relationship requires that engineers deal justly with both contractors and clients.

The consulting engineer often has an interest in maintaining good relationships and an excellent reputation with representatives of contractors and suppliers. Such representatives often provide leads to future work. Nevertheless, relationships with representatives of contractors and suppliers must remain highly ethical. Representatives should not be encouraged to feel that they have any special favors coming to them because of a long-standing relationship with the consulting engineer.

Several ethical responsibilities relating to contractors and suppliers are listed here.

- Plans and specifications must be definite and specific.

- Contractors are not required to furnish materials or do work not clearly called for in the contract documents.

- The consulting engineer requires that the contractor perform completely to the provisions of the contract and plans.

- The engineer does not unduly delay the contractor.

- The engineer assists in interpreting the plans and specifications in a fair manner.

- The engineer does not accept or solicit gifts, free engineering assistance, or other valuable considerations from suppliers.

4. DEALING WITH OTHER ENGINEERS

Consulting engineers should try to protect the engineering profession as a whole, to strengthen it, and to enhance its public stature. The following items will guide the engineer.

- The consulting engineer should not attempt to injure the professional reputation, business, or employment position of another engineer.

- The consulting engineer should not review someone else's work while the other engineer is still employed, unless the other engineer is made aware of the review.

- The consulting engineer should not try to replace another engineer once the other engineer has received employment.

- The consulting engineer should not use the advantages of a

PROFESSIONAL PUBLICATIONS, INC., P.O. Box 199, San Carlos, CA 94070

salaried position to compete unfairly with other engineers who would have to charge more for the same consulting services.

The above guidelines do not include a prohibition on competitive bidding. Until 1971, most codes of ethics considered *competitive bidding* detrimental to public welfare, since cost cutting would normally result in lower design quality. Therefore, ethical codes contained sections forbidding engineers to submit price proposals competitively.

In 1971, the Department of Justice declared that section in the National Society of Professional Engineers (NSPE) code of ethics to be in violation of Section One of the Sherman Antitrust Act. NSPE contended that the restraint of trade created by this ethics code was justified because competition among engineers was not in the public interest. The lower courts and all appeals through the U.S. Supreme Court failed to agree.

Although design professionals are still individually free to refrain from the practice of competitive bidding, professional societies are no longer allowed to require such restraint. Therefore, non-competitive bidding clauses are no longer present in codes of engineering ethics.

5. DEALING WITH THE PUBLIC

The relationship between an engineer and the public is essentially straight-forward. Responsibilities to the public demand that the consulting engineer place service to mankind above personal gain. Furthermore, proper ethical behavior requires that a consulting engineer avoid association with projects that are contrary to public health and welfare, or are of questionable legal character.

PROFESSIONAL PUBLICATIONS, INC., P.O. Box 199, San Carlos, CA 94070

PROFESSIONAL PUBLICATIONS, INC., P.O. Box 199, San Carlos, CA 94070

PART IV: CASE STUDIES OF ILLEGAL AND UNETHICAL BEHAVIOR

The following case studies are actual instances that have been judged illegal and/or unethical by the state in which the engineer worked. You should identify the codes and laws that prohibit such activities in your state.

Case Study 1. A professional engineer affixed his signature and seal to plans, designs, and drawings that were not prepared by him or prepared under his responsible direction, supervision, or control.

Case Study 2. A land surveyor placed advertising that tended to convey the impression that he was a professional engineer.

Case Study 3. A professional engineer affixed his seal and signature to a subdivision plat without staking the area in the field.

Case Study 4. A professional engineer was found to have performed engineering services before he became fully registered.

Case Study 5. A non-registrant acted as an engineering representative of a consulting engineering firm at municipal meetings.

Case Study 6. Four individuals opened an engineering consulting firm even though none of them was a licensed engineer.

Case Study 7. A land surveyor permitted employees to be in responsible charge of land surveying, and he failed to check the field procedures of his survey crew.

Case Study 8. A professional engineer relied on the information furnished by a grading contractor when certifying the grading.

Case Study 9. An employee of a professional engineer's firm altered the engineer's soils report without permission to do so.

Case Study 10. A professional engineer entered into a contract with a client, but later assigned the work to another firm without notifying the client.

Case Study 11. A professional engineer set a monument tagged with another person's certificate number.

Case Study 12. A professional engineer licensed in one state practiced for over a year in another state without a second license.

Case Study 13. An engineer continued to practice civil engineering even though he had not paid his annual dues for several years.

Case Study 14. An automobile repair shop operated under a name with the word "engineering" in it.

Case Study 15. A land surveyor submitted and filed numerous plats containing errors and omissions.

Case Study 16. A professional engineer was convicted of a felony totally

PROFESSIONAL PUBLICATIONS, INC., P.O. Box 199, San Carlos, CA 94070

unrelated to his engineering practice.

Case Study 17. A non-registrant had business cards printed with the title "Consulting Engineer" on them.

Case Study 18. A professional engineer used calculations prepared by another professional engineer without the second engineer's consent or knowledge.

Case Study 19. A professional engineer accepted money from a supplier while being employed by a client who was directed to purchase the supplier's products.

Case Study 20. Two professional engineers designed beach-site condominiums that collapsed during construction, killing several workers.

Case Study 21. A land surveyor failed to place his seal on various documents he recorded.

Case Study 22. A professional engineer testified in a court of law as an expert witness regarding a branch of engineering he was not licensed to practice in.

Case Study 23. A professional engineer changed plans bearing the seal of another professional engineer without certifying the changes with a second engineer's stamp.

Case Study 24. A professional engineer used the term "and Associates" in his company name even though there were no associates.

Case Study 25. The original founder of an engineering consulting firm bearing his name died. The remaining employees continued company operation under the name of the deceased partner.

Case Study 26. A professional civil engineer designed the electrical distribution system in a large building under his direction.

Case Study 27. A professional engineer failed to apply his signature and seal to an accoustical engineering report prepared under his supervision by an unlicensed person.

Case Study 28. An individual listed himself in the telephone directory yellow pages under the category of "engineer" although he had no license.

Case Study 29. A professional engineer wrote equipment specifications naming a company in which the engineer held a major stock interest.

Case Study 30. A professional engineer contracted to do surveying work for a client. The work was actually done by a licensed land surveyor without the knowledge of the client.

Case Study 31. A professional engineer changed the locations of monuments in the field without marking the changes on a filed map.

Case Study 32. A professional engineer certified that a county access road was 4 feet wider than it actually was.

PROFESSIONAL PUBLICATIONS, INC., P.O. Box 199, San Carlos, CA 94070

Case Study 33. A professional engineer continued to use his seal on plans prepared by others after his license had expired.

PROFESSIONAL PUBLICATIONS, INC., P.O. Box 199, San Carlos, CA 94070

PROFESSIONAL PUBLICATIONS, INC., P.O. Box 199, San Carlos, CA 94070

APPENDIX

TYPICAL CODE OF ETHICS *

PREAMBLE

Engineering is an important and learned profession. The members of the profession recognize that their work has a direct and vital impact on the quality of life for all people. Accordingly, the services provided by engineers require honesty, impartiality, fairness, and equity, and these services must be dedicated to the protection of the public health, safety and welfare. In the practice of their profession, engineers must perform under a standard of professional behavior that requires adherence to the highest principles of ethical conduct on behalf of the public, clients, employers and the profession.

I. FUNDAMENTAL CANONS

Engineers, in the fulfillment of their professional duties, shall:

1. Hold paramount the safety, health, and welfare of the public in the performance of their professional duties.

2. Perform services only in areas of their competence.

3. Issue public statements only in an objective and truthful manner.

4. Act in professional matters for each employer or client as faithful agents or trustees.

5. Avoid improper solicitation of professional employment.

II. RULES OF PRACTICE

1. Engineers shall hold paramount the safety, health, and welfare of the public in the performance of their professional duties.

    a. Engineers shall at all times recognize that their primary obligation is to protect the safety, health, property, and welfare of the public. If their professional judgment is overruled under circumstances where the safety, health, property, or welfare of the public are endangered, they shall notify their employer or client and such other authority as may be appropriate.

    b. Engineers shall approve only those engineering documents that are safe for public health, property, and welfare in conformity with accepted standards.

    c. Engineers shall not reveal facts, data, or information obtained in a professional capacity without the prior consent of the client or employer except as authorized or required by law or by this Code.

    d. Engineers shall not permit the use of their name or firm name nor associate in business ventures with any person or firm that they have reason to believe is engaging in fraudulent or dishonest business or professional practices.

e. Engineers having knowledge of any alleged violation of this Code shall cooperate with the proper authorities in furnishing such information or assistance as may be required.

2.   Engineers shall perform services only in the areas of their competence.

a. Engineers shall undertake assignments only when qualified by education or experience in the specific technical fields involved.

b. Engineers shall not affix their signatures to any plans or documents dealing with subject matter in which they lack competence, nor to any plan or document not prepared under their direction and control.

c. Engineers may accept an assignment outside of their fields of competence to the extent that their services are restricted to those phases of the project in which they are qualified, and to the extent that they are satisfied that all other phases of such project will be performed by registered or otherwise qualified associates, consultants, or employees, in which case they may then sign the documents for the total project.

3.   Engineers shall issue public statements only in an objective and truthful manner.

a. Engineers shall be objective and truthful in professional reports, statements, or testimony. They shall include all relevant and pertinent information in such reports, statements, or testimony.

b. Engineers may express publicly a professional opinion on technical subjects only when that opinion is founded upon adequate knowledge of the facts and competence in the subject matter.

c. Engineers shall issue no statements, criticisms, or arguments on technical matters that are inspired or paid for by interested parties, unless they have prefaced their comments by explicitly identifying the interested parties on whose behalf they are speaking, and by revealing the existence of any interest the engineers may have in the matters.

4.   Engineers shall act in professional matters for each employer or client as faithful agents or trustees.

a. Engineers shall disclose all known or potential conflicts of interest to their employers or clients by promptly informing them of any business association, interest, or other circumstances that could influence or appear to influence their judgment or the quality of their services.

PROFESSIONAL PUBLICATIONS, INC., P.O. Box 199, San Carlos, CA 94070

b. Engineers shall not accept compensation, financial or otherwise, from more than one party for services on the same project, or for services pertaining to the same project, unless the circumstances are fully disclosed to, and agreed to, by all interested parties.

c. Engineers shall not solicit or accept financial or other valuable consideration, directly or indirectly, in connection with work for employers or clients for which they are responsible.

d. Engineers in public service as members, advisors, or employees of a governmental body or department shall not participate in decisions with respect to professional services solicited or provided by them or their organizations in private or public engineering practice.

e. Engineers shall not solicit or accept a professionsl contract from a governmental body on which a principal or officer of their organization serves as a member.

5. Engineers shall avoid improper solicitation of professional employment.

a. Engineers shall not falsify or permit misrepresentation of their, or their associates', academic or professional qualifications. They shall not misrepresent or exaggerate their degree of responsibility in or the subject matter of prior assignments. Brochures or other presentations incident to the solicitation of employment shall not misrepresent pertinent facts concerning employers, employees, associates, joint venturers, or past accomplishments with the intent and purpose of enhancing their qualifications and their work.

b. Engineers shall not offer, give, solicit, or receive, either directly or indirectly, any political contribution in an amount intended to influence the award of a contract by public authority, or that may be reasonably construed by the public of having the effect or intent to influence the award of a contract. They shall not offer any gift, or other valuable consideration in order to secure work. They shall not pay a commission, percentage, or brokerage fee in order to secure work except to a bona fide employee or bona fide established commercial or marketing agencies retained by them.

III. PROFESSIONAL OBLIGATIONS

1. Engineers shall be guided in all their professional relations by the highest standards of integrity.

a. Engineers shall admit and accept their own error when proven wrong and refrain from distorting or altering the facts in an attempt to justify their decisions.

b. Engineers shall advise their clients or employers when they believe a project will not be successful.

PROFESSIONAL PUBLICATIONS, INC., P.O. Box 199, San Carlos, CA 94070

c. Engineers shall not accept outside employment to the detriment of their regular work or interest. Before accepting any outside employment, they will notify their employers.

d. Engineers shall not attempt to attract an engineer from another employer by false or misleading pretenses.

e. Engineers shall not actively participate in strikes, picket lines, or other collective coercive action.

f. Engineers shall avoid any act tending to promote their own interest at the expense of the dignity and integrity of the profession.

2.   Engineers shall at all times strive to serve the public interest.

a. Engineers shall seek opportunities to be of constructive service in civic affairs and work for the advancement of the safety, health, and well-being of their community.

b. Engineers shall not complete, sign, or seal plans and/or specifications that are not of a design safe to the public health, and welfare and in conformity with accepted engineering standards. If the client or employer insists on such unprofessional conduct, they shall notify the proper authorities and withdraw from further service on the project.

c. Engineers shall endeavor to extend public knowledge and appreciation of engineering and its achievements and to protect the engineering profession from misrepresentation and misunderstanding.

3.   Engineers shall avoid all conduct or practice that is likely to discredit the profession or deceive the public.

a. Engineers shall avoid the use of statements containing a material misrepresentation of fact or omitting a material fact necessary to keep statements from being misleading, statements intended or likely to create an unjustified expectation, statements containing prediction of future success, statements containing an opinion as to the quality of the engineers' services, or statements intended or likely to attract clients by the use of showmanship, puffery, or self-laudation, including the use of slogans, jingles, or sensational language or format.

b. Consistent with the foregoing, engineers may advertise for recruitment of personnel.

c. Consistent with the foregoing, engineers may prepare articles for the lay or technical press, but such articles shall not imply credit to the author for work performed by others.

4.   Engineers shall not disclose confidential information concerning the business affairs or technical processes of any present or former client or employer without his consent.

PROFESSIONAL PUBLICATIONS, INC., P.O. Box 199, San Carlos, CA 94070

a. Engineers in the employ of others shall not without the consent of all interested parties enter promotional efforts or negotiations for work or make arrangements for other employment as a principal or to practice in connection with a specific project for which the engineer has gained particular and specialized knowledge.

b. Engineers shall not, without the consent of all interested parties, participate in or represent an adversary interest in connection with a specific project or proceeding in which the engineer has gained particular specialized knowledge on behalf of a former client or employer.

5.   Engineers shall not be influenced in their professional duties by conflicting interests.

a. Engineers shall not accept financial or other considerations, including free engineering designs, from material or equipment suppliers for specifying their product.

b. Engineers shall not accept commissions or allowances, directly or indirectly, from contractors or other parties dealing with clients or employers of the engineer in connection with work for which the engineer is responsible.

6.   Engineers shall uphold the principle of appropriate and adequate compensation for those engaged in engineering work.

a. Engineers shall not accept remuneration from either an employee or employment agency for giving employment.

b. Engineers, when employing other engineers, shall offer a salary according to professional qualifications and the recognized standards in the particular geographical area.

c. Engineers in sales employment shall not offer or give engineering consultation, or designs, or advice other than that specifically applying to the equipment being sold.

7.   Engineers shall not compete unfairly with other engineers by attempting to obtain employment or advancement or professional engagements by taking advantage of a salaried position, by criticizing other engineers, or by other improper or questionable methods.

a. Engineers shall not request, propose, or accept a professional commission on a contingent basis under circumstances in which their professional judgment may be compromised.

b. Engineers in salaried positions shall accept part-time engineering work only at salaries not less than that recognized as standard in the area.

c. Engineers shall not use equipment, supplies, laboratory, or office facilities of an employer to carry on outside private practice without consent.

PROFESSIONAL PUBLICATIONS, INC., P.O. Box 199, San Carlos, CA 94070

8. Engineers shall not attempt to injure, maliciously or falsely, directly or indirectly, the professional reputation, prospects, practice or employment of other engineers, nor indiscriminately criticize other engineers' work. Engineers who believe other engineers are guilty of unethical or illegal practice shall present such information to the proper authority for action.

    a. Engineers in private practice shall not review the work of another engineer for the same client, except with the knowledge of such engineer, or unless the connection of such engineer with the work has been terminated.

    b. Engineers in governmental, industrial, or educational employ are entitled to review and evaluate the work of other engineers when so required by their employment duties.

    c. Engineers in sales or industrial employ are entitled to make engineering comparisons of represented products with products of other suppliers.

9. Engineers shall accept personal responsibility for all professional activities.

    a. Engineers shall conform with state registration laws in the practice of engineering.

    b. Engineers shall not use association with a non-engineer, a corporation, or partnership, as a "cloak" for unethical acts, but must accept personal responsibility for all professional acts.

10. Engineers shall give credit for engineering work to those to whom credit is due, and will recognize the proprietary interests of others.

    a. Engineers shall, whenever possible, name the person or persons who may be individually responsible for designs, inventions, writings, or other accomplishments.

    b. Engineers using designs supplied by a client recognize that the designs remain the property of the client and may not be duplicated by the engineer for others without express permission.

    c. Engineers, before undertaking work for others in connection with which the engineer may make improvements, plans, designs, inventions, or other records that may justify copyrights or patents, should enter into a positive agreement regarding ownership.

    d. Engineers' designs, data, records, and notes referring exclusively to an employer's work are the employer's property.

11. Engineers shall cooperate in extending the effectiveness of the profession by interchanging information and experience with other engineers and students, and will endeavor to provide opportunity for the professional development and advancement of engineers under their supervision.

PROFESSIONAL PUBLICATIONS, INC., P.O. Box 199, San Carlos, CA 94070

a. Engineers shall encourage engineering employees' efforts to improve their education.

b. Engineers shall encourage engineering employees to attend and present papers at professional and technical society meetings.

c. Engineers shall urge engineering employees to become registered at the earliest possible date.

d. Engineers shall assign a professional engineer duties of a nature to utilize full training and experience, insofar as possible, and delegate lesser functions to subprofessionals or to technicians.

e. Engineers shall provide a prospective engineering employee with complete information on working conditions and proposed status of employment, and after employment will keep employees informed of any changes.

* "Typical Code of Ethics" reprinted from publication 1102, "Code of Ethics for Engineers," National Society of Professional Engineers, 1420 King Street, Alexandria, VA 22314.

PROFESSIONAL PUBLICATIONS, INC., P.O. Box 199, San Carlos, CA 94070

ANSWERS TO REVIEW PROBLEMS

Part I

1. The written instrument is not negotiable. The instrument is payable only to John Smith, and not to order or to bearer. Unless the instrument specifies that payment is to be made to the order of some designated person or to the holder of the instrument, the instrument cannot be negotiable. In addition, though the instrument contains the date of signature, it does not specify a date of maturity. That is, the instrument does not state when the $150 obligation is to be paid. Without a statement that the money is payable on demand or at a designated time, the instrument cannot be negotiable. (negotiability, p. 39)

2. The written instrument is not negotiable. The instrument is payable only to John Smith, and not to order or to bearer. Unless the instrument specifies that payment is to be made to the order of some designated person or to the holder of the instrument, the instrument cannot be negotiable. (negotiability, p. 39)

3. The written instrument is negotiable. The instrument contains all the properties required for negotiability. The instrument is in writing, is properly signed by George Brown (maker), and is payable in a definite sum of money ($100). The instrument contains an unconditional promise to pay designated persons, and is to be paid on a specified date of maturity (six months after November 10, 19xx, the date of signature). Because the $100 is payable to Smith, White, Jackson, or order, the money can be paid to any one of them. In addition, the instrument can be negotiated by any one of the designated persons so long as that person possesses the instrument. (negotiability, p. 39; Uniform Commercial Code section 3-116)

4. The written instrument is not negotiable. Payment of the $100 depends upon whether John Smith ever marries. If John Smith does not marry, the $100 will never be paid. Because the condition of marriage is attached to payment, the instrument does not contain an unconditional promise to pay, and the instrument cannot be negotiable. (negotiability, p. 39).

5. The payee loses. When a bank certifies a check, it accepts the obligation to pay the amount of the check to the payee. At this point, the drawer is released from all liability to the payee. If the bank fails and cannot pay any of its obligations, the payee cannot sue the drawer for the amount owed and must take the loss. If the check had not been certified before the bank failed, the payee would have been able to sue the drawer. Until the bank certifies the check and accepts the obligation to pay, the drawer is liable to the payee for the amount of the check. (checks, p. 40; Uniform Commercial Code section 3-411)

6. A check does not need to be written in ink to be negotiable. The requirements for negotiability do not specify that an instrument

must be written in ink. Typed checks, printed checks, and checks written in pencil all meet the requirement that a negotiable instrument must be in writing. (negotiability, p. 39; Uniform Commercial Code section 1-201 (46))

7.   The check would remain negotiable. Because the words "or to anyone he designates" mean substantially the same as "or order," the unconditional promise to pay a designated person is not affected by the substituted wording. (negotiability, p. 39; Uniform Commercial Code section 3-110)

8.   The check is negotiable. "One cent" is a sum of money sufficiently definite to meet the requirements of negotiablity. (negotiability, p. 39)

9.   The check is negotiable. A check made payable to the order of John Smith or his agent is payable only to the principal (John Smith), but the agent may act as the holder of the check in place of the principal. The agent need not be named, and the word "agent" applies to all agents of John Smith acting within the scope of their authority. (negotiability, p. 39; agency, pp. 29-30; Uniform Commercial Code section 3-110)

10.   The promissory note is negotiable. January 1, 2000, is the date of maturity of the note. That is, the amount of the note is payable on January 1, 2000. A calendar date of maturity meets the requirement that a negotiable instrument be payable at a specified time. (negotiability, promissory notes, p. 39)

11.   The drawer is liable to the payee for the amount of a bill of exchange until the drawee accepts it. If the drawee fails to pay on the bill of exchange, the payee may sue only the drawer for the amount due. (bills of exchange, p. 40)

12.   A bank draft is a bill of exchange. Generally, a bank draft is an unconditional written order by one bank (as drawer) directed to another bank (as drawee) to pay a third party. The order is based on a business relationship between drawer and drawee, which usually consists of the drawer bank having deposits in the drawee bank. The bank draft works just like a check, and the rules applicable to checks are just as applicable to bank drafts. (bills of exchange, checks, p. 40; 11 Am. Jur. 2d 43-44)

13.   A bank draft that correctly meets all the requirements for negotiability does not need to be presented for acceptance before it becomes negotiable. Certain drafts have a requirement that they must be presented to the drawee for acceptance before they can be paid. A draft which must be presented for acceptance is negotiable during the period before it is presented to the drawee. (negotiability, p. 39; bills of exchange, p. 40; 11 Am. Jur. 2d 816-819)

14.   Failure to present a check for payment within a reasonable time relieves the drawer from liability. A check that is not certified and that is not a bank draft must be presented for payment within thirty days of the date stated on the check or within thirty days

of the date of issue, whichever is later, in order for the drawer to be liable for the amount of the check. (checks, p. 40; Uniform Commercial Code section 3-503 (2))

15. The last transaction between Jones and Smith discharged the instrument without having to take the check to the bank. If a person makes out a check payable to someone else, and later the check is endorsed back to the original maker, all intervening parties are released from liability, and the check is discharged. In other words, Smith cannot later sue Brown or Jones for payment of the debt owed to him, because endorsement of the check to Smith constituted actual payment of the debt, not just a promise to pay. (checks, p. 40; Uniform Commercial Code section 3- 208)

16. Berman bears the loss. Because he took temporary possession of the pictures for the specific purpose of framing, Berman is a bailee. As such, Berman is absolutely liable for the damage to the pictures occurring while the pictures were in his possession. (bailments, pp. 37-38)

17. Carson cannot remove the machinery. By mortgaging his property to Jordan, Carson has given Jordan a lien on the property as security for repayment of a loan of money. Assuming that the mortgage included construction of the new building, Jordan has a security interest in all items that became part of the new building during construction. Since the heavy machinery and boilers became fixtures in the building during construction, Jordan is entitled to the fixtures upon Carson's default in paying the mortgage. (mortgages, p. 24; fixtures, pp. 45-46; Uniform Commercial Code section 9-313(6))

18. The screens belong to Nelson. Because the screens can be easily removed from the house without causing any damage, they would be considered personal property belonging to Nelson. In addition, screens installed by Nelson for his own comfort during warm weather would be considered domestic fixtures, which also would belong to Nelson. Gardner would be entitled to the screens only if both parties understood that sale of the house included ownership of the screens. (fixtures, pp. 45-46)

19. If Bob can demonstrate that he had title to the topcoat before he lost it, he can compel Lynn to surrender the coat. However, the demonstration of title must consist of something more than mere identification of the coat. A showing that Bob had prior possession of the coat would be sufficient for recovery. Lynn can keep the coat if Bob fails to establish title. (title, pp. 31-32; 66 Am. Jur. 2d 845-847)

20. O'Leary does not get good title. In a consignment transaction, the consignor retains title to the goods until they are either sold to third parties or returned to the consignor. The consignee serves as a middleman to conduct sales to third parties. In this case, Barnett as consignee was authorized to act as Kaiser's agent for the sale of the transformers. Kaiser gave Barnett specific instructions to wait until the special agent arrived before selling any goods. When Barnett sold the transformers to O'Leary, he was not acting

within the scope of his authority, and title could not pass to O'Leary. Kaiser can sue to have his transformers returned. (agency, pp. 29-30; title, p. 31-32; 67 Am. Jur. 2d 144-150)

21.   Ketchum bears the loss. If not expressed in a contract, title passes when the goods are delivered. Since the person who holds title generally bears the risk of loss, it is important to determine when delivery takes place. Ketchum never delivered the poles to City Electric, and title never passed. The loss falls on Ketchum. Even if City Electric had marked the 50 poles with crayon, Ketchum would still bear the loss. As long as Ketchum retains possession of the poles, he holds title and bears the risk of loss. (title, pp. 31-32)

22.   Brady's statements constitute an express warranty. Before Gardner purchased the refrigerator, Brady represented to Gardner that the refrigerator would run "as quietly as a watch" and use "almost no energy." These statements are a clear guarantee of the machine's performance and cannot be dismissed as mere sales hype. As long as the refrigerator's performance is substantially different from Brady's warranty, Gardner can sue for breach of warranty and recover damages. (conditions and warranties, pp. 32-33)

23.   Lewis can sue for breach of warranty. In this sale by sample, Lewis bought 50 tons of gravel on the basis of a small sample. By supplying the sample for inspection, Acme created an express warranty that the 50 tons would correspond with the small sample. Because the 50 tons were substantially different in quality from the small sample, Lewis can sue on the breach. (conditions and warranties, pp. 32-33)

24.   Charles can resell all 100 cases. Because 50 cases are in transit and have not yet been delivered to Giese, Charles retains title to these cases and can resell them at will. In addition, Charles can resell the 50 cases in the packing house, which are in Charles' immediate possession. Charles probably could not sue the bankrupt Giese for breach of contract, because Giese would have no money to pay damages. (rights of seller and buyer, pp. 33- 34)

25.   In this case, Charles would have to sue to recover possession of the 50 cases. Once the cases were delivered to Giese, Giese acquired title to the grapefruit. Because Giese is bankrupt, Charles cannot really sue Giese for the price of the goods, because Giese has no money. Charles' only recourse is to sue to recover possession, in which case he must compete with all Giese's other creditors in court. Because the transaction was never completed, Charles would have priority as to possession of the grapefruit. (rights of seller and buyer, pp. 33-34)

26.   Norman can sue Thomas for breach of contract. Thomas did not accept the goods as offered, and the goods were undamaged. Norman can sue for the damages resulting from the breach, which in this case would be the difference between the contract price with Thomas and the actual sale price to Richard. Norman can recover the difference between 20 cents per pound and 15 cents per pound (5 cents per pound) multiplied by 100 pounds, or a total of $50.

PROFESSIONAL PUBLICATIONS, INC., P.O. Box 199, San Carlos, CA 94070

(rights of seller and buyer, pp. 33-34)

27. Because Barrett delivered the wrong quantity of goods to Wallace, Wallace has the option to accept or reject the shipment. If Wallace rejects the shipment, he can sue Barrett for damages resulting from the delay. If Wallace accepts the shipment, he can sue Barrett for any discrepancy in the value of the goods delivered and the price paid. In addition, Wallace has the option to accept only the portion of the goods for which he contracted. He can then send back the rest and sue Barrett for the costs of shipment, for damages resulting from delay, and for the value of the goods missing from the shipment. (rights of seller and buyer, pp. 33-34)

28. Reiner should sue Mathews for breach of contract. Once a seller has met his contractual obligation to deliver the goods as ordered, the buyer is required to accept the goods and pay for them. In this case, Mathews inspected the goods and informed Reiner that Reiner's obligation was complete. By refusing to accept the motors, Mathews has breached the contract and is liable to Reiner for damages. (rights of seller and buyer, pp. 33-34)

29. The plaintiffs lose. An advertisement for bids is only an invitation to entertain offers. Once an offer is submitted in response to the advertisement, the advertiser has the right to accept or reject the offer at will. In fact, the school board inserted a provision in their advertisement expressly stating that they reserved the right to reject. The plaintiffs' bid constituted an offer, which was rejected by the school board. Because there was no acceptance, the contract was not binding, and the plaintiffs cannot recover. (offer and acceptance, pp. 11-13)

30. Allen cannot hold Conrad to the offer. An offer must be directly communicated by the offeror to the offeree in order to be accepted. There can be no contract if a third party informs the offeree of the offeror's intentions, unless the third party has been authorized by the offeror. In this case, Miller informed Allen of Conrad's intent to make an offer without authority from Conrad. Allen cannot accept Conrad's offer unless Conrad directly communicates the offer to Allen or authorizes an agent to do so. (offer and acceptance, pp. 11-13)

31. Baxter may not hold Jason to any offer. An offer must be definite and must express contractual intent in order to be accepted. Jason's statement is not definite. He suggests that he might be interested in selling in the future, but makes no clear offer to Baxter that, if accepted, would effect a binding contract. Because Jason's statement does not express any definite intent to sell, it does not constitute an offer, and Baxter cannot create a binding contract by accepting. (offer and acceptance, pp. 11-13)

32. The offer to sell "some cement" would not be a legal offer. The terms are too vague, and the parties could not understand or agree to the terms of such an offer based only on such indefinite wording. If, however, both parties understood the price and amount of cement from prior conversation or correspondence, then the contract could be enforceable. (offer and acceptance, pp. 11-13)

PROFESSIONAL PUBLICATIONS, INC., P.O. Box 199, San Carlos, CA 94070

33.   Collins can recover from Jackson. Jackson breached his contract
      with Collins by failing to remove the wheat from the field. If Col-
      lins performs Jackson's obligation without any apparent protest
      against the breach, Collins' action could constitute a waiver of
      performance, excusing Jackson from liability for the breach. How-
      ever, as long as Collins expressly reserves his rights against Jack-
      son, he can sue Jackson for the breach and recover damages. In
      this case, damages include the cost to remove the wheat. (breach
      of contract, pp. 19-21; 17 Am. Jur. 2d 835-837)

34.   Green can hold Jones to the offer. Because the offer was made
      by mail, acceptance became effective at the moment Green drop-
      ped his letter in the mailbox. If Green's acceptance had not
      become effective, Jones' offer would have been revoked at the
      moment Green received the telegram. Since acceptance preceded
      revocation, Green has a contract with Jones. (offer and accep-
      tance, pp. 11-13)

35.   (a) Acceptance is binding. The letter was mailed and received
      before the time period for acceptance had expired. (b) Acceptance
      is binding. Because the offer was made by mail, acceptance
      becomes effective at the moment a letter of acceptance is drop-
      ped in the mailbox. In this case, the fact that Campbell's office
      received the letter before the time period had expired indicates
      that Bowman had mailed the letter before expiration. Acceptance
      became effective once the letter was mailed. (c) Acceptance is
      binding if the letter was mailed before the time period expired. It
      does not matter when Campbell actually received the letter. (d)
      Acceptance is binding. If Bowman had received Campbell's letter
      of revocation before he posted the letter, the revocation would
      have become effective at the moment Bowman received the letter.
      However, because Bowman posted the letter first, acceptance
      became effective at the moment it was mailed, and the revocation
      has no effect. (offer and acceptance, pp. 11-13)

36.   (a) The acceptance is binding. The telegram was sent and received
      before the time period for acceptance had expired. (b) The accep-
      tance is not binding. Because the offer was communicated by
      mail, acceptance by telegram is not effective until received. Since
      the telegram was not received until after the time period for accep-
      tance had expired, the acceptance is not binding. (c) The acceptance
      is not binding. It does not matter when the telegram reaches the
      telegraph office in the city of destination. Because the telegram
      was received by Campbell after the time period had expired, the
      acceptance is not binding. (d) The acceptance is binding. Camp-
      bell's office serves as his agent for the receipt of business
      communications. Because his office received the telegram before
      the time period for acceptance expired, the acceptance is binding.
      It does not matter when Campbell himself actually sees the tele-
      gram. (offer and acceptance, pp. 11-13)

37.   (a) The acceptance is not binding. Sellens cannot require Atkins to
      furnish 25 cream-colored refrigerators merely because he adds this
      requirement to his acceptance. Because the request for cream-col-
      ored refrigerators is a substantial modification to Atkins' offer,

Sellens' reply constitutes an independent counter-offer. If Atkins accepts the counter-offer, his acceptance would be legally binding. (b) Atkins did not have the right to dispose of the refrigerators before June 10. In his offer to Sellens, Atkins expressly stated that the offer would be open until June 10. Though Atkins had the right to revoke his offer at any time, he did not give Sellens notice of revocation before Sellens accepted the offer. Sellens' acceptance is legally binding, and Atkins can be held liable for failure to provide the refrigerators. (offer and acceptance, pp. 11-13).

38. Hoit's acceptance is not binding. Revocation is effective when received by the offeree. When offer and acceptance are both made by telegram, acceptance is binding upon dispatch. Although Hoit dispatched his acceptance at 12:15 p.m. before seeing the revocation at 1:30 p.m., his office received the revocation at 11:30 p.m. Since revocation was received before acceptance was dispatched, the revocation became effective first, and Hoit's acceptance was not binding. (offer and acceptance, pp. 11-13)

39. Keefer cannot recover for breach of contract. Standing alone, the words "you are the lucky man" are too vague to constitute acceptance. Without some express statement of acceptance or some obvious act from which acceptance can be reasonably inferred, Keefer has no justification for interpreting the president's vague statement as an acceptance. Since AC did not accept Keefer's offer, there was no contract, and Keefer cannot recover. (offer and acceptance, pp. 11-13)

40. Martin can collect from Rossen. Rossen committed a partial breach of contract by failing to have the building ready by March 1. If Martin performs Rossen's obligation without any apparent protest against the breach, Martin's action could constitute a waiver of performance, excusing Rossen from liability for the breach. However, as long as Martin expressly reserves his rights against Rossen, he can sue Rossen for the breach and recover damages. In this case, damages include the cost to remove the cases. (breach of contract, pp. 19-21; 17 Am. Jur. 2d 835-837)

41. (a) Jacobs cannot collect from Warner for the price of the suit. Unless Warner somehow caused the damage to Jacobs' suit, he cannot be liable for negligence. In addition, Jacobs can be considered to have assumed any risk of damage, since he did voluntarily stop to assist Warner. By willingly and knowingly taking an unnecessary risk, Jacobs absolved Warner of any liability. (b) Jacobs cannot recover medical expenses from Warner. Although personal injury is a much more serious tort than damage to property, the liability is still the same. Warner cannot be liable for negligence unless he somehow caused the injury. In addition, Jacobs assumed the risk of injury, since he voluntarily stopped to assist Warner. By willingly and knowingly taking an unnecessary risk, Jacobs absolved Warner of any liability. (negligence, pp. 36-37)

42. Gessit Company cannot collect from AC Power Company for breach of contract. Acceptance of an offer must be communicated to the offeror in some way before the acceptance can become effective. Though AC Power may have decided internally to

accept Gessit's offer, it never communicated its acceptance to Gessit either by formal response or by performance. Without some sort of formal acceptance, the parties could not be bound by the contract, and Gessit could not recover for breach of contract. (offer and acceptance, pp. 11-13)

43. Farmer Brown cannot sue to collect the reward. He apprehended and turned over the suspect to the police before he had any knowledge of the reward. Because a person cannot accept an offer of which he is ignorant, there is no acceptance and no binding contract. Thus, Brown cannot sue to compel payment if the offeror fails to pay the reward. However, nothing prevents Farmer Brown from collecting the money if the offeror voluntarily pays him. (offer and acceptance, pp. 11-13)

44. If Benson's father used duress or undue influence in order to induce young Benson to deed the land over to him, the contract would be voidable. In addition, the contract may not be binding as a result of the grossly disproportionate consideration. Young Benson deeded $8,000 worth of land to his father for only $2,000. If Benson had been simple-minded or old and weak-minded, he would not have had the legal capacity to make a contract. If one party is not capable of understanding the terms of the contract, the fact of mental incapacity prevents the contract from being legally binding. The contract with Sherman would not be binding for lack of definite consideration. Assuming Benson's father is not dead, Benson's rights to his father's estate are intangible and subject to change. For example, Benson could receive much of his father's estate as a gift while his father is still alive and then not even be mentioned in his father's will. In this circumstance, Sherman would receive nothing for the value of Benson's rights. Because Benson's rights to his father's estate are intangible, they cannot serve as proper consideration, and the contract is not binding. (voidable contracts, pp. 9-10; consideration, pp. 13-15; legal capacity, p. 16)

45. The defense of mistake will not work. Mistake is not a valid reason for voiding a contract when one party makes a mistake and the other party does not know about it. Pascalli did not know that Madsen needed a rug with a brown background and not a blue background, and no fraud was involved in the transaction. Since Madsen merely made a bad deal, he cannot be excused from the contract. (17 Am. Jur. 2d 492-494)

46. Frank's defense was good. If both Frank and Compson relied upon the assumption that zoning laws permitted conversion of the house into a two-family residence as a material basis for making the contract, the mutual mistake would make the contract voidable, and Frank would not be obligated to perform on the contract. (voidable contracts, pp. 9-10; 17 Am. Jur. 2d 490)

47. Corey would not be successful in a suit charging fraud. Though Simon may have misrepresented the value of the stock in order to make the sale, Corey has suffered no damage. Corey made enough on resale of the stock to meet whatever interest he could have earned with the money in a bank. If Corey had not sold the

stock, he could have recovered the price he paid plus interest from Simon. Because Corey made enough off the sale of the stock, he cannot sue Simon for more money. (voidable contracts, pp. 9-10)

48. The note is not binding. Because the father was compelled to sign the note under duress, the contractual obligation represented by the note cannot be enforced. In addition, the consideration offered by the bank is illegal. In return for the father signing the note, the bank offers to withhold information concerning a felony from the authorities. An agreement to obstruct justice is contrary to public policy and cannot be enforced. (voidable contracts, pp. 9-10; legality, pp. 16-17)

49. The children would have to go to court to have the land transfer invalidated. If the children could prove that the young man used duress or undue influence to induce Miss Ritter to deed the land, the land contract would be voidable. In addition, if Miss Ritter was not capable of understanding the terms of the contract because of her advanced age, she would not have the legal capacity to make a contract, and the fact of her mental incapacity would prevent the land transfer from being legally binding. (voidable contracts, pp. 9-10; legal capacity, p. 16)

50. Sam can recover against John for fraud. Though John made no statement to Sam about the model of the car, Sam relied upon the false information that John told Rick and Rick told Sam. Since John intended for Sam to rely upon the false information transmitted to Rick, John had the requisite intent to deceive. Because Sam bought John's car on the basis of John's misrepresentation of material fact, Sam can sue John in tort for damages. (misrepresentation, p. 36; 37 Am. Jur. 2d 252-253)

51. Moore could not be liable for fraud. Since no one knows how the city will eventually develop, speculation as to the future expansion of the city could not reasonably be interpreted as a statement of fact but rather would be seen as a matter of opinion. Because Smith relied on an expression of opinion instead of on a material misstatement of fact, he is liable for his own mistake and cannot recover from Moore. (misrepresentation, p. 36; 37 Am. Jur. 2d 73-75)

52. (a) If both Hoffman and Turner relied upon the assumption that the dog was three years old as a material basis for the contract, the mutual mistake would make the contract voidable, and Turner could get his money back. (b) The fact that Turner knew about Hoffman's mistake does not make the contract invalid. In the absence of a duty to disclose, the fact that a party knows that the other party is making a mistake is not fraudulent, even though the other party may be relying on the mistake as a reason for making the transaction. The law does not excuse "bad deals" just because one party makes a mistake. Thus, the contract is binding. (c) The contract is binding. A party cannot recover for fraud or misrepresentation without some showing of actual damages. If Turner did not suffer any damages, the contract remains valid. (d) If Hoffman makes his statement without any intention of defrauding any particular individual, he cannot be liable for fraud.

PROFESSIONAL PUBLICATIONS, INC., P.O. Box 199, San Carlos, CA 94070

However, if the parties relied upon the assumption that the dog was three years old as a material basis for the contract, the mutual mistake would make the contract voidable. (e) For recovery on the basis of either fraud or mutual mistake, a plaintiff must show that the statement in issue was relied on in order to agree to the contract. If the statement in question had no role in the decision to contract, it does not matter whether the statement was fraudulent or mistaken. Since Turner cannot show that the statement in any way influenced his decision to buy, he would be denied recovery on the basis of fraud or mistake. (voidable contracts, pp. 9- 10; misrepresentation, p. 36; 17 Am. Jur. 2d 490-494; 37 Am. Jur. 2d 255-256, 297-299)

53. Simpson had the right to refuse for lack of consideration. Lewis had already installed the outlets as consideration for the first agreement. Because past consideration cannot be used as consideration for a new contract, Lewis' services could not be used as consideration for Simpson's services under the second agreement. For the second contract to be binding, Lewis must offer some independent consideration, such as a promise to install more outlets or to forego the cost of materials incurred under the first contract. Without independent consideration, Simpson is not obligated to furnish services to Lewis. (consideration, pp. 13-15).

54. There is no binding contract between Kerr and Denton. Contracts to obtain the reduction of a criminal penalty by influence or pressure are invalid as against public policy. Since Kerr offered to give Denton the contract for rewiring Kerr's new house in exchange for Denton's influence in getting a reduction of Kerr junior's speeding fine, the consideration offered by Denton is illegal, and the contract is void. Even though Denton may have used his influence to help the Kerr boy, he cannot compel Kerr to fulfill his part of the illegal contract. (legality, pp. 16-17; 17 Am. Jur. 2d 577)

55. Martin gets the desk, and McFadden gets $20. Martin accepted McFadden's offer, and the ensuing contract is legally binding. McFadden would argue that the consideration was unequal: $20 is not an equal exchange for a desk valued at $100. If the consideration were grossly disproportionate to the value received, a court might refuse to enforce the contract. In this case, $20 does not sound "grossly disproportionate" but rather just seems like a bad business deal. Courts will not disallow contracts just because one party exercised bad judgment. In addition, the $100 estimate is merely Boswell's opinion. This one opinion standing alone is probably not sufficient to establish the value of the desk. (consideration, pp. 13-15).

56. O'Hennessey's defense is good. A promise to refrain from exercising a legal right is considered a legal detriment and can be used as consideration for a binding contract. The changing of O'Casey's name is a legal detriment, since the act involves giving up the legal right to use any other name but O'Hennessey. However, the detriment of changing one's name to O'Hennessey may not compare with the immense value of O'Hennessey's estate offered in exchange. A court would most likely determine that the legal detriment suffered by O'Casey is grossly disproportionate to the value

PROFESSIONAL PUBLICATIONS, INC., P.O. Box 199, San Carlos, CA 94070

of O'Hennessey's fortune and would refuse to enforce the contract. (consideration, pp. 13-15)

57. Bob cannot recover the balance of the original debt. When Bob accepted Joe's secured note for $4,000, a new contract was formed. Bob forfeited his rights to the full $8,000 as consideration for Joe's note. When the note was paid and the mortgage was satisfied in accordance with the agreement, Joe fulfilled his obligation to Bob. Bob is required by contract to fulfill his end and forfeit the balance of the original debt. If Joe had failed to pay his note on time, he would have breached the contract, and Bob would not have been obligated to forgive the debt. In this case, Bob would have been able to sue for payment of the full $8,000 under the terms of the original agreement. (consideration, pp. 13-15)

58. Galt cannot recover the extra $250. The administrator of an estate has the power to settle claims against an estate. Therefore, Fisher was operating within his power by offering $750 to Galt in exchange for Galt releasing his claim on Kerock's estate. When Galt accepted the offer for $750, a new contract was formed. Galt forfeited all rights to the $1,000 as consideration for the $750. Because the new contract was binding, Galt no longer has any grounds to sue on the old claim. (consideration, pp. 13-15; 31 Am. Jur. 2d 136)

59. Harper cannot recover against Milton. Harper committed a criminal act by trying to pay Milton to refrain from testifying, and he can be criminally liable for attempting to bribe a witness and obstructing justice. If Milton had fulfilled his part of the bargain, he too could be prosecuted for obstructing justice. Courts will not enforce contracts for the commission of crimes, and thus the contract between Harper and Milton is not enforceable. (legality, pp. 16-17)

60. Hugh Dow cannot prevent Seidel from starting the same kind of business in the same state. Contracts in restraint of trade or competition are unenforceable as a matter of public policy. Since Dow's contract with Seidel attempts to restrain competition between the two businesses, it cannot be enforced, and Dow would lose any lawsuit alleging breach of contract by Seidel on these grounds. (legality, pp. 16-17)

61. Jones would lose his lawsuit. Although Acme may have violated a statute in fulfillment of its contractual obligation, the violation has nothing to do with the terms of the original contract. The contract between Acme and the city was made for a legally valid purpose and had sufficient consideration to support it. Once Acme completed the sewer and the city accepted it, the city was contractually bound to fulfill its part of the bargain and pay the $50,000. Acme might be fined for violating the statute, but the violation itself would not lead to breach or invalidation of the contract. (legality, pp. 16-17)

62. The trial judge ruled incorrectly. Because the refrigerators conceivably could be sold and the contract completed before a year had

passed, the contract is not covered by the section of the Statute of Frauds requiring contracts to be in writing if they would take more than a year to complete. Thus, the oral contract was binding, and Holmes should have recovered damages. The appellate judge ruled correctly. The agreement does fall within the section of the Statute of Frauds requiring contracts to be in writing if they involve sales of goods in excess of $50. Holmes' contract with Glass involved the sales of goods in excess of $50, since the contract would not be completed until all 500 refrigerators were sold, resulting in a sales value of $75,000. Because the contract was not in writing, it was not enforceable under the Statute of Frauds. The supreme court was incorrect in ruling for Holmes. Because the contract fell within the section of the Statute of Frauds requiring contracts to be in writing if they involve sales of goods in excess of $50, the oral contract was unenforceable as a matter of law. Holmes is entitled to compensation for the benefits he rendered to Glass during the three month period, but he should not have recovered any other damages resulting from the breach. (oral and written contracts, p. 9; 72 Am. Jur. 2d 670)

63. Billingsley would not be able to force Haskins to live up to his agreement. A court will not order specific performance of a contractual obligation when specific performance will cause hardship or injustice for one of the contracting parties. If a court ordered Haskins to allow Billingsley to dig and haul away ore, Haskins would be denied the use of his mine for other purposes, and the court order would constitute an unfair taking of Haskins' mine without Haskins' consent. Instead of specific performance, a court most likely would make Haskins pay damages to Billingsley. Damages would consist of the machinery and preparation costs incurred by Billingsley prior to operating the mine. (breach of contract, pp. 19-21)

64. The question of Bass' liability depends upon the laws of the state in which the oil well sits. If the state considers Bass' contract an oil lease, and if it considers an oil lease an interest in real property, the oral contract would come under the Statute of Frauds and would not be enforceable. In this event, Bass would be excused from liability. On the other hand, if Bass' contract is considered a sale of oil instead of a lease, or if the state does not consider an oil lease an interest in real property, then the oral contract would not be covered by the Statue of Frauds and would be enforceable. In this situation, Bass would be liable to Brown for any damages resulting from the breach of contract. (oral and written contracts, p. 9; 38 Am. Jur. 2d 541-542; 72 Am. Jur. 2d 648-649)

65. The Statute of Frauds would not be a very good defense. The personal service contract between Carmichael and McCoy does not fall within any of the traditional forms of contracts covered under the Statute of Frauds. Unless the Statute of Frauds specifically requires Carmichael's type of personal service contract to be in writing, then the oral contract between Carmichael and McCoy would be enforceable. If Carmichael cannot plead a better defense, he will liable to McCoy for damages resulting from breach of contract. (oral and written contracts, p. 9)

PROFESSIONAL PUBLICATIONS, INC., P.O. Box 199, San Carlos, CA 94070

66. Johnson must show that the contract between himself and Acme was binding, that Acme breached the contract, and that Johnson suffered damages as a result of the breach. The terms of the contract must be clear, or else the contract will be rendered unenforceable, and Johnson will lose. Because the plaintiff bears the burden of proof in this type of suit, Johnson cannot recover from Acme if he cannot produce evidence sufficient to prove these three elements in court. (contracts, p. 5; interpretation of contracts, pp. 17-18; breach of contract, pp. 19-21; 17 Am. Jur. 2d 897-898)

67. (a) Lee's order constitutes an offer to buy 100 lamps from Clark. Clark showed his acceptance of Lee's offer by tendering two lamps as partial performance, which Lee accepted. Lee's acceptance of the two lamps showed that Lee received and understood that Clark had accepted his offer, and thus Lee can be held to his order. (b) Clark's act of giving Lee the kitchen-lamp unit is unconnected with the terms of the offer. It cannot be construed as acceptance of the offer, and Lee can revoke at any time. (c) Clark is able to produce evidence that an offer was made, but he has made no attempt to accept the offer. Until Clark accepts either by formal response or by performance, Lee may revoke the offer at any time. (d) Though Lee has made an advance payment on his offer, Clark has yet failed to accept Lee's offer. The advance payment gives Lee the right to sue Clark for return of the money, if Clark does not accept the offer. It does not give Clark the right to hold Lee to his offer. Lee can revoke his offer at any time before Clark accepts, and then sue to recover his advance payment. (offer and acceptance, pp. 11-13; 67 Am. Jur. 2d 193-199)

68. Lift Elevator would be required to remove the elevator. Lift made an express warranty to Clifton that if the elevator was not completely satisfactory to Clifton, Lift would remove the elevator at its own expense. The terms of the warranty are very clear, and as long as Clifton relied on the warranty as a basis for contracting with Lift, Lift is required to meet the terms of the warranty. It does not matter whether the elevator was installed in accordance with the best engineering practice. If Lift fails to remove the elevator, Lift can be liable to Clifton for damages resulting from the breach of warranty. Damages most likely would consist of the cost of removal. (conditions and warranties, pp. 32-33)

69. The contractor could be liable for breach of contract for failing to follow the contract specifications, substituting 4-inch drains for 6-inch drains. The contractor could also be liable for negligence if any damage to person or property occurs as a result of negligent installation of the 4-inch drains. Negligence and breach of contract cases are generally tried in state court, and Clinton would have to prove damages as a result of Broderick's substitution. For example, damages could consist of the cost of replacing the 4-inch drains with 6-inch drains. Clinton can recover only once for Broderick's error, and thus would elect to sue on the contract theory or the tort theory depending on which was easier to prove and which would provide the most damages. (breach of contract, pp. 19-21; negligence, pp. 36-37)

70. Roades cannot be held for breach of contract. Acme made a partial

PROFESSIONAL PUBLICATIONS, INC., P.O. Box 199, San Carlos, CA 94070

breach of contract by indefinitely postponing Roades' start after June 1. If Roades had not done anything but sit at home, he could have sued Acme for any damages he suffered by not working from June 1 until he started with Acme. However, Roades was responsible for minimizing any damages resulting from Acme's breach if he had the opportunity. Accepting the position with Boeing was such an opportunity, and Roades cannot be required to breach his contract with Boeing when he accepted the job in order to minimize Acme's breach. Acme either will have to wait until Roades is finished with Boeing or will have to cancel its contract with Roades and hire someone else, in which case Roades will be able to sue Acme for total breach of contract. (breach of contract, pp. 19-21)

71. Eazy Oil cannot compel specific performance from Lindley but can recover damages from him. A court will not order specific performance of a contractual obligation when specific performance will cause hardship or injustice for one of the contracting parties. If a court required Lindley to fulfill his part of the contract by continuing to design the 25 stations, the requirement of performance would amount to forced labor, since Lindley chose not to work on the Eazy Oil project. Yet Lindley committed a total breach of contract by assigning his rights to Glascoe. Eazy Oil could sue Lindley for any losses incurred as a result of Lindley's breach. (breach of contract, pp. 19-21)

72. B & O must pay damages to Gotham City for breach of contract. If a contract becomes impossible to complete, the terms are no longer binding on the parties. However, if a party enters into a contract and then performs some act that makes the contract impossible to complete, the party that performs the act cannot use impossibility as a defense to escape performance on the contract. Thus, B & O cannot claim impossibility, since B & O built the retaining wall that made the contract impossible to complete. If B & O had asserted impossibility before it built the retaining wall, the defense would have been successful as long as it was impossible to eliminate the grade crossing without decreasing the width of the street. (discharge of contract, pp. 18-19; 17 Am. Jur. 2d 856)

73. Though the agent may have been acting within the scope of his authority, a principal does not have to reimburse the agent for damages suffered by reason of the agent's own misconduct. Thus, a principal does not have to reimburse his agent for a criminal fine incurred because the agent ran a red light. (agency, pp. 29-30; 3 Am. Jur. 2d 613)

74. The principal is liable if the accident occurred while the agent was acting within the scope of the contract between agent and principal. For example, if the agent's truck skidded while in the process of delivering the principal's goods as required by contract, the truck would have been operating within the scope of the contract when the accident occurred, and the principal would be liable. If, however, the truck had been off-duty or transporting cargo belonging to a third party, it would not have been operating under the contract when the accident occurred, and the principal would not be liable. (agency, pp. 29-30)

PROFESSIONAL PUBLICATIONS, INC., P.O. Box 199, San Carlos, CA 94070

75. The principal would not be required to fulfill the agreement. A principal is bound by the acts of his agent only if those acts are committed within the scope of the agency contract. If an agent is specifically instructed not to make a certain type of agreement, the authority to make such an agreement is not included within the scope of the agency contract. Thus, a principal would not be required to fulfill such an agreement, regardless of whether the third party had any knowledge of the agent's instructions. (agency, pp. 29-30)

76. The principal would be required to fulfill the agreement. Green was empowered to sell Smith's truck. In the absense of specific instructions not to trade the truck for another vehicle, the authority to trade the truck for value is within the scope of Green's agency contract with Smith. Since a principal is bound by the acts of his agent if the acts are committed within the scope of the agency contract, Smith would be bound by the agreement to trade his truck for Brown's car. (agency, pp. 29-30)

77. Taylor can hold Earle for the spoiled goods. A principal is deemed by law to have knowledge of any facts that his agent knows and should have communicated to the principal, regardless of whether the principal actually knows the information. Thus, Earle is liable for not collecting the goods until May 31, even though he did not know that the goods were ready on May 23. Because Earle's agent knew that the goods were ready to deliver, Earle is liable for the loss. (agency, pp. 29-30; Restatement 2d of Agency section 272)

78. Lindsey can be held personally liable to Winter for damages. An agent is required to execute his duties to the principal with due care and skill. If Lindsey was negligent in selecting the particular type of motors to run the paper mills, he could be liable to Winter for breach of contract or for negligence in tort. In addition, if Lindsey misrepresented his background in order to secure the agency contract with Winter, he could be liable for fraud. (agency, pp. 29-30; tort, pp. 35-38)

79. Cox does not have to pay the $300 to Cornell. If a contract becomes impossible to complete, the terms are no longer binding on the parties. It became impossible for Cornell to fulfill his end of the contract, since the house was destroyed by fire and could no longer be sold. Thus, the contract was no longer binding between Cornell and Cox, and Cox was no longer required to pay Cornell. (discharge of contract, pp. 18-19)

80. The judge was correct in ruling that Smythe was liable. By testifying under oath that Cutter was his agent in Center City, Smythe led third parties to believe that Cutter had the apparent authority to act as Smythe's agent in Center City. As long as Wallace relied in good faith upon Smythe's own representation that Cutter was Smythe's agent, Smythe is liable for any contract entered into by Cutter as Smythe's agent. Thus, Smythe is liable for his defective shingles, regardless of whether Cutter ever was his agent by formal contractual agreement. (agency, pp. 29- 30; 3 Am. Jur. 2d

477)

81. Smith would be successful in his suit to enforce the contract. Ratification occurs when a principal affirms a contract with a third party made by an agent who acted without the authority to make such a contract. Ratification makes the contract between principal and third party binding, as if it had been authorized by the principal at the outset. Although Brown was not authorized to act as Smith's agent when he entered into the agreement with White, Smith's ratification of the contract made the contract binding between Smith and White. By refusing to fulfill his part of the agreement, White breached a binding contract and is liable for damages. (agency, pp. 29-30; Restatement 2d of Agency section 82)

82. (a) McKay does not have the authority to purchase unnecessary land. If Acme suffers any damages, McKay can be liable for breach of contract or for negligence, since he acted beyond the scope of his authority. If the sale of the land is voided, McKay can be liable to the landowner for damages under the theory that he breached an implied warranty to purchase the land in his capacity as Acme's agent. Acme is not bound by the terms of the contract. (agency, pp. 29-30; Restatement 2d of Agency section 329) (b) McKay does not have the authority to keep the balance of the $500,000. By keeping the money, McKay has violated his fiduciary duty to Acme and is liable to Acme for the amount withheld. In addition, McKay could be criminally prosecuted for embezzlement. (agency, pp. 29-30) (c) The general rule is that an agent cannot delegate authority to a subagent unless the principal consents. Since Acme did not consent to hire Richards for the actual buying of the property, McKay is not acting within the scope of his authority by hiring Richards and can be liable to Acme for breach of contract or for negligence. In addition, Richards may sue McKay for compensation under the employment contract, even though Acme is not bound by the contract. If Richards were employed to perform only mechanical or ministerial acts, McKay would be authorized to hire him without Acme's consent. Since negotiation and purchase of property are not merely mechanical or ministerial acts but rather are substantive aspects of McKay's duties, Acme's consent is required to hire Richards. (agency, pp. 29-30; Restatement 2d of Agency section 78; 254 F.2d 283) (d) Miller resembles Richards in situation (c). Since an agent cannot delegate authority to a subagent unless the principal consents, McKay is acting beyond the scope of his authority by hiring Miller. In this case, McKay gives Miller even more substantial responsibilities than he gave Richards. Miller is not performing merely mechanical or ministerial acts, and thus McKay will be held liable for lack of Acme's consent. McKay can be liable to Acme for breach of contract and for negligence and can be sued by Miller for failure to perform on an employment contract. Acme is not bound by the contract with Miller. (agency, pp. 29-30; Restatement 2d of Agency section 78; 254 F.2d 283) (e) McKay acted beyond the scope of his authority when he purchased the property for $600,000. Yet Acme cannot just start using the property and then not pay McKay because he failed to follow his instructions. By retaining the benefits of McKay's purchase, Acme ratifies by conduct McKay's act of purchasing the property and can be held liable to McKay for the extra $100,000.

(agency, pp. 29-30; 3 Am. Jur. 2d 560-562) (f) In this case, Acme never accepted the benefits of McKay's purchase. Since McKay acted beyond the scope of his authority, Acme is not bound by the purchase and can sue McKay for breach of contract and for negligence. In addition, McKay could be liable to the landowners from whom he purchased the property for any damages resulting from the failed sale. (agency, pp. 29-30; Restatement 2d of Agency section 329) (g) McKay can hire Carson as a chainman without Acme's consent, since Carson is not responsible for a substantive part of McKay's duties, but rather only for the mechanical functions of a chainman. Yet because McKay hired and delegated some of his duties to Carson, McKay is liable to Acme for any breaches of duty committed by Carson. In addition, Carson as a subagent has the same responsibilities to McKay as McKay has to Acme. Therefore, Carson would be liable to McKay for any damages suffered by McKay as a result of Carson's bad mistake. (agency, pp. 29-30; Restatement 2d of Agency section 428) (h) If Carson was hired for purely mechanical duties or with Acme's consent, Acme as principal will be liable to Johnson for the lost cow. Under the doctrine of respondeat superior, an employer is liable for all torts committed by his employees within the scope of employment. Acme will be liable only if a tort was actually committed. Therefore, if Carson really was not negligent, no one would be liable for the death of the cow, and Johnson would have to take the loss. (agency, pp. 29-30; 3 Am. Jur. 2d 631-632) (i) Carson was not acting within the scope of his employment when he entered Johnson's house to steal the watch. Since an employer can be held liable under respondeat superior only for acts of employees operating within the scope of employment, neither McKay nor Acme would be liable for the value of Johnson's watch. Of course Carson would be both criminally and civilly liable for the theft. (agency, pp. 29-30; 53 Am. Jur. 2d 463) (j) Since McKay is injured while acting within the scope of employment, his injury would be covered by the state workmen's compensation statute. Acme is required to carry workmen's compensation insurance, which would cover the cost of McKay's claim for relief. (agency, pp. 29-30; negligence, pp. 36-37)

83. All the defendants sued by the injured passerby could be liable somehow for the tort. Mapes would not be liable under respondeat superior for the injury. Though the contractor and his employees were operating within the scope of their employment when the injury occurred, the very nature of the relationship between an independent contractor and his employer presumes that the employer really has no control over the project, leaving all responsibility to the contractor. Thus, the general rule is that the employer will not be liable. However, Mapes could be liable for his own negligence in selecting the particular contractor. Jones, the contractor, would be liable for the injury. An employer can be held liable under respondeat superior for injuries caused by acts of employees operating within the scope of employment. In addition, Jones could be liable for negligence in hiring the operator of the equipment, if he hired someone unqualified for the job. The engineer and the foreman could be liable for their own negligence in failing to supervise the operator of the equipment. The operator himself could be liable for his own negligence in permitting the

PROFESSIONAL PUBLICATIONS, INC., P.O. Box 199, San Carlos, CA 94070

equipment to overheat. If the equipment had some kind of design or manufacturing defect that caused overheating and injury, the equipment-renting company could be liable under strict liability in tort. (negligence, pp. 36-37; strict liability, p. 62; 41 Am. Jur. 2d 774-781; 53 Am. Jur. 2d 410-411)

84. Baxter would be excused from the contract. In a contract for personal services in which only one particular person can perform the project, death or serious illness would render the contract impossible to perform, and the terms would no longer be binding on the parties. When Baxter became incapacitated by the serious heart attack, his contract with Balin became impossible to complete, and Baxter was no longer bound by the contract. (discharge of contract, pp. 18-19)

85. Lawson can compel Seacole to take back the engine and refund the money. If both Lawson and Seacole relied upon the assumption that the engine would deliver 50 brake H.P. as a material basis for making the contract, the mutual mistake would make the contract voidable, and Lawson could sue to get his money refunded. If Seacole intentionally or negligently misrepresented the horsepower capacity of the engine, Lawson could sue for breach of contract or for tort to get his money back plus damages. (voidable contracts, pp. 9-10; misrepresentation, p. 36; 17 Am. Jur. 2d 490)

Part II

1. Under the Wright v. Winterbottom precedent, the window washer would not be able to sue the design engineer. Because the design engineer contracted with the building owner and not the window washer, the window washer had no prerequisite of privity between himself and the engineer. That is, the window washer had no face-to-face contractual relationship with the design engineer. Without a direct relationship, the engineer would not be liable for the window washer's injury. Modern day courts would apply the doctrine of strict liability in tort, making the design engineer liable if a design defect in the construction of the building was the cause of the injury. For the window washer to recover, he would have to prove the design of the building was defective, that the injury was caused by the defective design, and that the activity during which the injury occured was a reasonably foreseeable use of the building. The window washer does not need to show any privity of contract between himself and the design engineer. (history, pp. 60-61; strict liability in tort, p. 62)

2. Bartlett would argue that because there is no privity of contract between himself and Kent, he cannot be liable. As a surveyor, Bartlett has a duty to exercise due skill and care in making the survey. This duty arises from the contract between Bartlett and Wisehart, and if Wisehart sued and Bartlett and failed to exercise due skill and care, Bartlett would be liable to Wisehart. Since Kent is not a party to the employment contract, Bartlett should not be liable to Kent. In addition, Bartlett's survey may not have been the cause of Kent's damages. Kent may have been negligent in

relying on Bartlett's survey or on Wisehart's representations without investigating the true facts. Kent may also have negligently paid off the new purchasers before liability had been determined. Kent won the case because the court determined that privity of contract was unnecessary for suit on Bartlett's breach of duty. Bartlett owed a duty of due care to all purchasers of the property who relied on his survey, and Kent could sue in tort for damages resulting from Bartlett's negligence. Thus, if Bartlett's survey was the cause of damages, and if Bartlett failed to exercise due to care and skill in preparing the survey, Bartlett would be liable to Kent. (negligence, pp. 36-37; 35 A.L.R.3d 504)

3.   The hotel did not have any grounds on which to base the suit. It could not sue on the basis of strict liability in tort, becuase there was no injury caused by a defect. Though the hotel wisely avoided its own liability by refusing to open the pier under unsafe conditions, it cannot sue for a tort if no injury has occured. In addition, the hotel could not sue on a breach of contract by the engineer. The design team was retained to design a pier for sunbathers. The only foreseeable use for such a design is to be used in good weather, whether by sunbathers, sightseers, or fishermen. Since the pier could not be used in bad weather, the design team could not be responsible if bad weather prevented opening of the pier. Though the hotel might argue that the engineer failed to perform on the contract because the pier could not be opened on time, the engineer could not be liable unless the contract expressly stated that design of the pier must facilitate sunbathing under all foreseeable weather conditions. (design defect, pp. 61-62; strict liability in tort, p. 62; breach of contract, pp. 19-21)

4.   The manuafacturer of the aerosol can was correct in arguing that the presence of a warning against incineration should excuse liability for the injury. If a product is inherently and unavoidably dangerous despite the present state of technology, the manufacturer should not be held to strict liability as long as users of the product have been sufficiently warned of potential dangers. The aerosol can contained a clear warning not to incinerate, and really the parents were negligent in allowing their child to play with an aerosol can near an open fire. The argument that the manufacturer should have developed a safe means of failure besides explosion is inadequate if the technology does not allow such a development. (warning notices, p. 66; 63 Am. Jur. 2d 788-791)

5.   In a suit for strict liability in tort, the designer and his company would not be liable. The designer and his company could be held liable only for design defect involving the entire connection, such as specifying the wrong type of fastener. Because the designer specified fasteners "of the highest quality and strength," the inadequate sampling plan apparently failed to reveal only defects in individual fasteners, rather than any defect in the design of the entire connection. The defect occurred in manufacture and not in design, and the designer and his company would not be liable. On the other hand, the fastener manufacturer would be liable. By testing only a sample rather than exhaustive testing, the manufacturer took the risk that some defective fasteners would slip through the precautions and cause failure. In a suit for strict liability, the

PROFESSIONAL PUBLICATIONS, INC., P.O. Box 199, San Carlos, CA 94070

manufacturer would be liable for injuries caused as a result of the manufacturing defect in the fastener. (manufacturing and design defect, pp. 61-62; strict liability, p. 62; safety, reliability, and quality, pp. 65-66)

6. The manufacturer should be held strictly liable for the death. The car had a defect in design when it was manufactured and when it was used. In addition, it is reasonably foreseeable that a driver would use his car to cross a set of raised railroad tracks. The manufacturer would be liable so long as the design defect caused the death. For example, if a train hit the car, killing the driver, as the car was trying to cross the railroad tracks, the manufacturer would be liable only if the cross member actually was caught on the tracks, forcing the car to stop. If the defect had no role in the accident, the manufacturer would not be liable. (strict liability, p. 62)

7. If it was reasonably foreseeable that the chemical insecticide would be used by non-English speaking workers, then the manufacturer was required to put warning labels in multiple languages on the inherently dangerous product. Since chemical insecticide is commonly used on farms, and since migrant farm workers often do not speak English, the manufacturer could likely expect that a non-English speaking worker might be injured by the product. If the manufacturer had included a skull and crossbones on the label, it could have avoided liability, since the skull and crossbones is an internationally understood symbol for poison. With only a message in English, the manufacturer failed to inform its users adequately and should be liable. (warning notices, p. 66)

8. The dismissal was appropriate. In the 18-year history of the whirlpool bath, it could have been inadequately serviced, improperly maintained, or unreasonably altered, so that the bath was much different in structure at the time of injury as it was on the date of installation. In addition, the bath may have had an effective life of only 10 years. The purpose of statutes of limitation is to protect the courts and defendants from stale claims, in which witnesses and evidence have become unreliable over time. Engineers and architects should be entitled to this protection, even though their products may still be used after the limitations period. However, the plaintiff still has a good case against the university and any service contractors for negligence in maintaining the bath over time. (strict liability, p. 62; negligence, pp. 36-37)

PROFESSIONAL PUBLICATIONS, INC., P.O. Box 199, San Carlos, CA 94070

INDEX

PROFESSIONAL PUBLICATIONS, INC., P.O. Box 199, San Carlos, CA 94070

PROFESSIONAL PUBLICATIONS, INC., P.O. Box 199, San Carlos, CA 94070

power, 4
power of attorney, 30
precedent law, 2
prescription, 43
primary rights, 4
primitive societies, 1
principal, 29
principle of estoppel, 31
private corporation, 27
product designers, 59
promise, 5
promisee, 39
promisor, 39
promissory note, 6, 38-39
proof of consideration, 41
public gatherings, 2
public nuisance, 36
punitive damages, 20

quality, 65
quasi-contract, 7
quitclaim deed, 42

real property, 22, 40
real property law, 40
real property mortgage, 24
recognizance, 6
reliability, 65
revoked, 13
reward, 12
right, 4

safety, 65
sale, 31
sale by sample, 33
secondary rights, 4
seller, 31
seller's lien, 34
several contract, 8
Sherman Antitrust Act, 71
sight draft, 40
sole proprietorship, 24
special damages, 20
special power of attorney, 30
specific performance, 20, 34
stare decisis, 2
state courts, 3
state law, 4
statute, 2
statute of frauds, 9

statute of limitations, 10
statutory law, 2
stock corporation, 27
strict liability in tort, 59, 62
subcontractor, 23
subjective intent, 11
Supreme Court, 3
Supreme Court decisions, 2-3

tax lien, 22
teasing, 36
tenant, 23
tender of performance, 20
terms of the agreement, 21
time draft, 40
title, 31
tort, 35
tort law, 35
total breach, 19
township description, 41
toxic waste, 36
trade fixtures, 46
traffic laws, 2
tribal customs, 1

ultra-vires acts, 28
unconditional contract, 6
undue influence, 10, 16
unenforceable contract, 10
Uniform Commercial Code, 31
Uniform Partnership Act, 25
unilateral contract, 7
United States legislature, 3

vendee, 31
vendor, 31
void contract, 10
voidable contract, 10, 16

warranty, 32
warranty deed, 41
warranty disclaimer, 33
wax seal, 7
workmen's compensation, 37
written contract, 9

zoning, 43
zoning ordinance, 2

PROFESSIONAL PUBLICATIONS, INC., P.O. Box 199, San Carlos, CA 94070

Quick – I need additional study materials!

Please rush me the review materials I have checked. I understand any item may be returned for a full refund within 30 days. I have provided my bank card number as method of payment, and I authorize you to charge your current prices against my account.

Solutions Manuals:

For the E-I-T Exam:
[ ] Engineer-In-Training Review Manual   [ ]
  [ ] E-I-T Quick Reference Cards
  [ ] E-I-T Mini-Exam with Solutions

For the P.E. Exams:
[ ] Civil Engineering Reference Manual   [ ]
  [ ] Civil Engineering Sample Exam with solutions
  [ ] Civil Engineering Quick Reference Cards
  [ ] Seismic Design
  [ ] Timber Design
  [ ] Structural Engineering Practice Problem Manual
[ ] Mechanical Engineering Review Manual   [ ]
  [ ] Mechanical Engineering Quick Reference Cards
[ ] Electrical Engineering Review Manual   [ ]
[ ] Chemical Engineering Review Manual
  [ ] Chemical Engineering Practice Exam Set
[ ] Land Surveyor Reference Manual   [ ]

Recommended for all Exams:
[ ] Expanded Interest Tables
[ ] Engineering Law, Ethics, and Liability

SHIP TO:

Name _____

Company _____

Street _____ Apt. No. _____

City _____ State _____ Zip _____

Daytime phone number _____

CHARGE TO (required for immediate processing):

_____ _____

VISA/MC/AMEX account number   expiration date

_____
name on card

_____
signature

Send more information

Please send me descriptions and prices of all available E-I-T and P.E. review books. I understand there will be no obligation.

_____
_____
_____
_____

A friend of mine is taking the exam too. Send additional literature to:

_____
_____
_____
_____

I disagree...

I think there is an error on page _____ . Here is the way I think it should be.

Title of this book: _____

[ ] Please tell me if I am correct.

Contributed by (optional):

_____
_____